The
Balanced
Leader

The
Balanced
Leader

TIM MCEWAN
& RODERIC YAPP

The Balanced Leader
by Tim McEwan and Roderic Yapp.

First published in Great Britain in 2021.
Copyright © Tim McEwan and Roderic Yapp 2021.

Tim McEwan and Roderic Yapp have asserted their right
under the Copyright, Designs and Patents Act 1988
to be identified as the authors of this work.

Copyediting by Hazel Bird.
Illustrations by Red Axe Design.
Cover image adapted from a photo by Kelly Sikkema.
Typesetting by Eleanor Abraham,
using Adobe Garamond Pro, Domus and Domus Titling.

email: info@balancedleaders.co.uk

www.balancedleaders.co.uk

ISBNs
Print: 978-1-9196423-0-7
eBook: 978-1-9196423-1-4

Dedication:

For Hannah, Charlotte and Harrison.

For Archie and Poppy.
Be everything you can be – have the spirit.

CONTENTS

PART TWO
SKILLS TO PERFECT THE RIGHT BALANCE EVERY TIME

INTRODUCTION

Leadership is an art, not a science. The art of balance – the subject of this book – means a leader regularly needs to decide on the right balance of activity, or emotion, needed to react to a particular situation.

I first became interested in the subject of balance when I was training as a cadet at the Royal Military Academy Sandhurst. As cadets, we hadn't yet been in the eye of the storm and we'd constantly bombard our instructors with questions. One particular question that came up very frequently was: what is the right distance to be away from our lead section? In other words, what is the right place for a leader to put themselves in the field of battle? The same answer invariably came back: 'a tactical bound'.

The phrase 'a tactical bound' meant as little to me back then as it probably does to you reading this now. It wasn't until we went on our final training exercise in Cyprus that I fully understood what it meant. We were doing a platoon attack through an olive grove. The nice thing about olive groves is that there is a flat stretch followed by a metre-high stone wall, followed by another flat stretch and another wall, and so on. It was the perfect setting for our purpose. I placed my lead section forward to assault, my fire support section off to my left, and my reserve section behind me. Even today, I can clearly remember

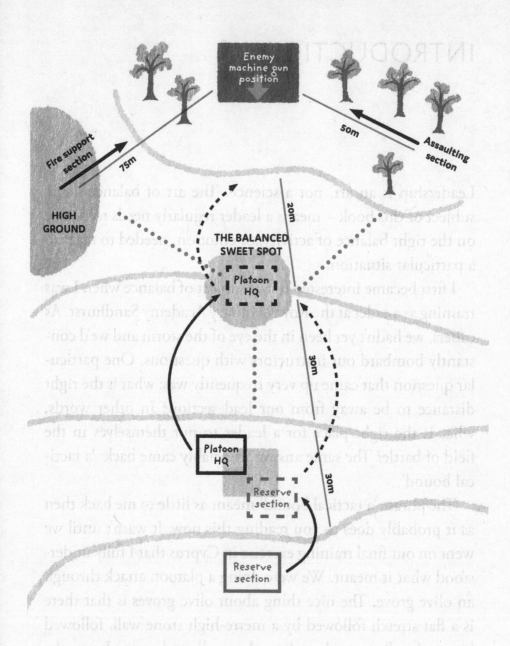

Figure 1. Sketched map of the situation in the olive grove.
I was positioned in Platoon HQ (PL HQ)

how that felt. At that moment in time, I felt completely in balance and in control of what was going on. If anything started to fail, I could shift to the right place really quickly. I had found the tactical bound. In this practical setting, I completely understood the importance of being in exactly the right place, with the right plan, at the right time. I have included a graphic in Figure 1 to help you visualise this.

Following my military career, and after spending some time working for various organisations, I moved on to run my own business coaching leaders. Again and again, when I was running workshops, people would ask: what is the best way to lead? The answer to the question was always: it depends. It depends on the situation. I realised then that I needed to go back to basics and find some way of explaining the virtues of balanced leadership and the tactical bound. I obviously didn't have the advantage of being able to take people on a military exercise, so instead I began to ask people to visualise a 1980s 'boom box' (Figure 2).

Figure 2. A 1980s 'boom box'

11

Now, this shows my age, so let me explain. These stereos were all the rage, and the bigger your machine, the more 'cool' you were. They had six or seven sliders, which altered certain elements of the sound. The sliders were referred to as a 'graphic equaliser', although technical sound engineers would disagree with that description. However, each apparently had its purpose. Of course, none of us knew what they did, and our settings often simply stayed in place regardless of the music we were playing, even though each different track might have benefited from a different setting.

Imagine a leadership quality being attributed to each slider. If our leadership settings are never changed (i.e. if we don't amend the settings according to what a particular situation demands), we are only ever in balance by chance. What would be far more effective would be for leaders to learn how to alter their leadership sliders to meet every unique situation, and balance themselves. Too much bass in a track that requires subtle high tones is going to sound awful. It's the same with a leader who uses a high degree of control when delegation and empowerment would be a far more effective approach.

In both music and leadership, there will never be any such thing as the *exact right level* that stays the same in perpetuity. What is right will change all the time and levels need to be constantly adjusted according to the circumstances. In leadership, this means an ebb and flow of leadership techniques based on an assessment of the situation at any given moment. It is really important for a leader to be able to balance their settings to meet different situations if that leader wishes to be as effective as they can be, for as much of the time as possible.

I met Roderic Yapp, an executive coach, in October 2016. He had a broadly similar military background to me; in his case, as a troop commander in the Royal Marines. I was interested to hear that he had come to the same conclusion as me about balanced leadership and that he strongly believed that success lies in a leader's ability to adapt their behaviour to suit the circumstances. In Roderic's case, his viewpoint was inspired by his training to become an executive coach after he left the services. He'd been told that there is a range of ways to help people move towards their goals, but, nearly always, they already have the answers within them. His job was to ask the right questions to lead them towards the changes in behaviour that would most suit the situation. Most importantly, the right behaviour would vary hugely for each situation. The fundamentals of our interactions – what we do in a given context and the outcomes generated (whether positive or negative) – dictate whether or not we are good leaders. It was not long before we began to work together, coaching leaders in the art of balanced leadership.

We are, we believe, offering a very different view of effective leadership from what you get elsewhere. Nearly all of the vast numbers of leadership books that have been written focus on one aspect of leadership. It might be courageous leadership, or creative leadership, or engaging leadership, or any one of hundreds of different approaches. Everything, in any given situation, is boiled down to relate to that key skill. The problem with this approach is that it is just too limiting. It may well have worked for that particular leader in a very specific situation. They may have, say, needed to take a tough leadership approach to enact a big change programme, or be an engaging leader to pull together a broken organisation. However, in our view, this linear approach won't work in every situation. Far from it. Things change. All the time. And leadership needs to react to that.

There is no single way of leading. When Roderic and I embarked on our military training, no one said to us: if you learn how to do such-and-such really well, you will be a good leader. That would have been ridiculous. When you get out into the field, things change at a rapid and unexpected pace, and you need to be able to react to that, or you and the people under your command will pay the ultimate price.

It is the same in less confrontational situations too. The one-size-fits-all leadership model does not take into account that the context changes. Some of the much-praised ways to be a good leader in today's world won't be appropriate in *every* circumstance. Likewise, styles of leadership that have been dismissed as old fashioned or out of date, such as the command-and-control style of leadership, may be relevant in some instances.

We have, as you will see, included many examples and stories throughout the book to help illustrate and bring to life the effectiveness, or otherwise, of balanced or imbalanced leadership. Let's begin by giving you one of them here. Say you and I meet up to go for a walk to discuss this balanced leadership thing. Along the way, we come across the aftermath of a terrible accident. A cyclist has been hit by a car and is lying in the road, alone and badly injured. The car and its driver are nowhere to be seen. The current vogue in leadership encourages discussion, agreement and empowerment among teams. Except, in this circumstance, the last thing you would probably want to me to do is say, 'Do you think it's a good idea to call an ambulance? Or do you think it would be better to knock on some doors to see if anyone saw anything?' Technically this would mean that I had empowered you to make decisions, but it is obvious that in this context this is a terrible way of taking charge of a time-crucial situation.

Leadership should be flexible and fit the environment. Most importantly, leadership behaviour is shaped by context. An example I often use is that the way you behave at a party is different from how you'd behave at a funeral. You are the same person, but the context has changed. Equally, it's less what you say and more how you act that inspires, engages and influences people to follow you. In the case of the cyclist's incident, it would be far better if I immediately adopted a command-and-control strategy and told you to go up the road to flag down cars to stop them driving into the scene, while I called the emergency services. That would be the way to start effectively controlling that particular situation. (Strangely, Roderic and I have both been first on the scene in similar situations and had to do just this.)

In this book we have focused on many different leadership approaches; whether it is diving into the detail, keeping a watchful eye on the big picture, or knowing how to judge when it is time to really challenge the team and when it is better to leave them to get on with it. We've discussed when it is better for a leader to be creative and when it is more effective to go by the book. Empathy is important; however, as we show, it's not always the best way to get things done. Occasionally, you need to be firm but fair. To help you visualise the range of different approaches, we've shown them on a series of spectrums, which demonstrate that the requirements of leadership change according to circumstances. We've highlighted six different spectrums but we are aware that in certain circumstances and specific occupations there may be others. If this is the case for you, you will easily be able to adapt the spectrums to your own circumstances using these six as a foundation. The point to remember is: any leader who sticks to one leadership style, come what may, will never get the most from their organisation. Flexibility is the key to good balance.

We completely understand that most people will, by and large, be comfortable with their style of leading, whether they tend to be more at the command-and-control end of things, or prefer a more empathetic, team-orientated approach. That's fine and perfectly natural. However, to achieve balance you also need to develop the skills to adjust to a different tack as and when required.

To help you achieve this and become more accomplished in skills that may not initially come naturally to you, Part Two of this book deals with teaching the fundamental foundations you need. Practise these skills often and they will soon become part of your day-to-day armoury. As a result, you will be able to shift your leadership up or down a gear, with ease, as and when required. It is worth noting that there is some overlap between the skills required, where you may, for example, need judgement, engagement and trust all at the same time. It is up to you to judge how much of each to deploy in any given situation. However, if you fully understand how to use each skill, it is much easier to make the right call.

Balance is a crucial component, if not *the* crucial component, in successful leadership. In today's fast-paced world, it is very easy to get into a situation of reacting to circumstances as they come along, one after another. However, that is not always the best strategy for either the short or the long term. Balanced leadership allows for a fluid reaction, but a more considered one too. It encourages leaders to be more purposeful, more situationally aware of events leading up to decision points, and more conscious of the range of issues to be solved, rather than of the one demanding immediate attention. Occasionally, this will entail pausing and taking time for reflection, before reframing the issue and solving it differently. Often, it will mean letting go of the notion that leaders always need to know all the answers straight away. Observing what other information is emerging may be a more effective course. This doesn't mean that a reaction is not required – it simply means that more time is given to choosing the *right* reaction.

Balance is the key to successful leadership.

CHAPTER ONE
BALANCE AND IMBALANCE

Looking back at all the major economic, political, business and environmental catastrophes over the past hundred years, there is one common factor that unifies them all. No, it is not greed – although that played a role. Nor is it self-interest – even though, again, that contributed.

It is balance. Or, more accurately, imbalance.

In the first few months of 2020, as the world gradually awoke to the coronavirus threat that was steadily and relentlessly creeping across the world, one of the first reactions came from the global stock markets, which plummeted by double-figure amounts, with trillions being knocked off the value of listed companies. Wall Street saw its fastest bear-market plunge in history. The Dow Jones industrial average of 30 leading US shares fell by more than 20% of its previous peak and more than eight years of gains on the FTSE100 were wiped out in a month. Traders were, of course, concerned that growth would stall and supply chains would be disrupted by lockdown measures being taken to contain the virus. This would, in turn, be bad for company profits, and a hit to profits translates into lower returns for shareholders. Yet, the sheer scale and speed of the sell-off also told another story. The market had been massively overheated and out of balance. Before the pandemic, stocks had been accelerating upwards for months, with no growth figures whatsoever to underpin the massive valuations. Something had to change, and individual traders acted quickly before it was too late.

While the market correction has since evened out considerably – and in some cases returned to pre-coronavirus levels (although it is still too early to judge the long-term economic effects of the pandemic) – it's not the first time we've seen these huge swings thanks to imbalance in the financial markets. The 2008 global credit crisis was also triggered by a correction to a market that was seriously out of balance. Somehow banks had allowed a bunch of exuberant financiers to get carried away with their claim that they could banish risk, when in actual fact they had simply lost track of it. A flood of irresponsible mortgage lending saw millions of loans doled out to subprime borrowers with poor credit histories and no cash to repay their debt. The mortgages were passed on to financial engineers, who chopped them up and redistributed them as pools of supposedly 'low-risk' securities. Big banks argued it would all be fine and it was – right up until the moment the property market slumped, throwing the loan pools out of whack and tipping everything on its head.

It's not just the financial markets where we've seen the extreme results of imbalance. It has also been at the root of some of the biggest corporate bankruptcies in history. When Enron collapsed in 2001, taking the dubious honour of the number one slot in this league table of enormous business failures prior to the banking collapses that followed the 2008/9 crises, it was found to have adopted some extraordinary accounting practices to hide billions of dollars in debts arising from poor deals. In all the enquiries that followed, one thing that was abundantly clear was that the company's leadership had pursued completely the wrong priorities. The balance was seriously skewed away from proper business practices.

Politically, throughout history we have seen the rise of parties that operate at the extreme ends of the political spectrum. This invariably happens in times of hardship or after periods of accelerated change. From the rise of the Nazi Party in the thirties to the current resurgence of the far right in Europe and the US, these are all signs of a fragmented, unstable and imbalanced environment. These are situations where extremism thrives.

In nature, there is one big balancing act going on, all the time. You only need to look at the current climate change situation and the damage being wreaked by unseasonable weather, with bush fires at one end and floods at the other. If the delicate balance of nature is disrupted by industrialisation, excessive waste and emissions, the consequences for the environment can be substantial and even threatening to the very existence of our species.

While the cases noted here are all extreme, the fact is that balance has an impact on every organisation and environment, large and small, whatever the sector. And it is led from the top.

Take the process of setting a vision for an organisation's future. Here, good balance is based on the delicate juggling act of being able to see the big picture and generate groundbreaking ideas, but also getting into the detail to make sure the ideas are realised by following through and working with the team. In each case, a leader has to be confident about operating at one extreme or another with ease. Any leader who is too focused on the tomorrow, but without really worrying about the today, is setting themselves up for a fall. Having a vision is good, but it needs to be balanced by attention to performance in real time. Performance requires a sense of direction and context, and a series of goals. And it's not just a case of setting goals and making sure everyone is on board and working towards achieving them either.

Balancing between overseeing the big-picture goals and getting into the detail is just one of numerous options that leaders need to master. There are many other different approaches that they need to quickly and effortlessly shift between as they adapt to constantly changing circumstances. At times they may need to be challenging, whereas on other occasions a bit of support will go a long way. Yes, leaders should lead from the front and be confident when making the tough decisions, but they also need to match these qualities with genuine humility. Sometimes they need to be sticklers for process, and at other times a bit of creativity is called for.

Leaders who stick to a linear model, doggedly applying one style of leadership for every situation, will see their organisation suffer. You may well recognise the classic signs of imbalance from places where you have worked in the past, or even from where you are now. The first, and clearest, signal of lack of balance is often found among the team. There will be a high turnover of staff, or the wrong turnover, where the stars all leave and the less effective employees stay. Another signpost to imbalance is when obvious silos appear. A particular department will wield the upper hand, or managers will withhold information or use fear as a key motivator. And it is an even bigger indication that things are heading in the wrong direction when leadership firmly gets behind a department like this, showing they value and recognise their efforts over and above those of everyone else. Others in the organisation are made to feel like second-class citizens. When a scenario like this is allowed to fester, the culture quickly becomes toxic.

Leaders who don't understand the need for balance tend towards having an emotional reaction to new circumstances, rather than a thoughtful and considered one. This is something else that is to the detriment of the whole organisation.

Imagine a situation where someone comes into the boss's office and admits that they haven't done a piece of work that they've been asked to do. In response, the boss immediately flies off the handle and berates the person for their lack of achievement. For good measure, the boss angrily lists other occasions when the employee has fallen short. This is not adapting to the circumstances in any way. It is just an emotional reaction, which also means that the boss has to pick up the pieces of whatever damage their outburst has done before anything constructive can be salvaged.

What should have happened here is for the boss to respond, 'Okay, well can you talk to me about why you haven't managed to complete the project?' It's far more constructive to dig beneath the surface to understand. With a thoughtful, controlled and measured response, there is a better outcome all round. At some point, if need be, that same boss could eventually get to a position where they could take the employee aside and calmly explain that the delay on the project was not acceptable and express their displeasure. If that is done in a considered manner, and balanced with an offer to guide the employee in the future if there is a sticking point, then it might be helpful to everyone. Lashing out doesn't get anyone anywhere and is a classic sign of an imbalanced organisation or individual.

Another clear indicator of imbalance within an organisation relates to overall direction. There may be much management speak about 'priorities', 'vision' and 'goals' but nothing really changes and no real pathway is set out towards realising these lofty pronouncements. Hardly surprisingly, cynicism will set in and then (ironically) these priorities will have even less chance of being actioned. Redressing the balance once things have gone this far is never easy.

Conversely, companies with balanced leadership thrive. They tend to grow faster and have better profit margins. Not surprisingly, balanced organisations regularly feature in 'best places to work' surveys. When jobs get advertised, they have plenty of applicants and the people who do get jobs will stay longer. Employees will talk proudly about where they work and will be able to articulate clearly and compellingly why their company is better.

The problem many leaders encounter is that they are who they are and find it almost impossible to change. They are absolutely fine dealing with issues that require one sort of characteristic – such as being decisive and confident – and hopeless when it comes to letting others have a say or showing a little humility. Frequently, leaders find it hard to let go and consistently ignore the feelings of those around them. Or, to put it even more simply, they can tend to be control freaks. They can't resist meddling in everything and this can be hugely frustrating for everyone around them, particularly if they are pretty sure they've got it covered. At the other end of the spectrum to the control freak leader is the boss who is more inclined to be a people person. They like to be liked and find it extremely difficult to be overly challenging. Neither leadership style is entirely right or wrong. They both have merits in certain situations. What is wrong is when a leader only ever plays to their strengths. If a leader is constantly riding their team hard to get things going and is forever hectoring them to get on with things, the team will have no time for peace and reflection and will soon become exhausted and dysfunctional. At the other end of the scale, imagine a jokey, let's-all-relax-and-have-fun type of leader. At first this might seem a refreshing way to get everyone motivated, but when does the humour stop and the real work begin?

No leader can adopt one way of leading and stick with it come what may. Balanced leadership is situational, depending on the needs of the organisation and the individuals within it at a particular moment in time. It is also subject to a huge range of external influences: from the trading environment to the wider economy to customer preferences to a looming threat from a new competitor. What seems important one day will not be a priority the next and vice versa. Each new scenario can and will affect balance and will require a quick response from the leadership. The style of that response may vary each time too, but the most important thing for balance is for a leader to pivot quickly and effectively.

Diversity is key to creating a balanced organisation, in terms of both gender and ethnicity. *Cognitive* diversity is crucial too. On the surface, you may judge that Roderic and I are very similar. We are both white men with a military background. We like to think that we're not quite pale, male and stale, but perhaps we are in some people's eyes! Scratch the surface, though, and you'll find that we're completely different. If you have a conversation with us, you will discover that we see the world in very different ways and operate within it differently too. Roderic generally veers towards the desire to control everything and follow strict processes. In fact, he is 100% about the process, and his day runs to a strict schedule which is written down in a series of neatly written notes. (He even does this on the weekend!) I'm always in awe of his organisational skills, but I recognise that I have strengths of my own. I am, for example, much more comfortable delegating and working creatively with teams to see what works best. While I plan my workshops carefully, I am flexible when it comes to letting situations develop and evolve.

Neither of our approaches is perfect – certainly not if we applied them to every single circumstance. Sometimes, though, they are spot on. The point here is that to be balanced leaders, we both need to find a way to embrace each other's characteristics on occasion. In our case, we've managed this feat by working together. When we do leadership seminars together, Roderic is great at coming up with details of various leadership approaches and researches vivid stories about them. When it comes to being creative and facilitating team exercises, it is over to me. It's a really effective way to shore up any areas where we are less confident or comfortable and achieve the perfect balance. It also shows the real value in building teams with different skills, where people operate at different ends of a given spectrum. Of course, that does mean the ultimate leader needs to have some humility and willingness to invite other ideas into the mix. However, if you leverage that balance, it has the potential to help any organisation become an absolute superpower.

A crucial first step towards balanced leadership is to do as Roderic and I have done: recognise your strengths and weaknesses and the impact your default state has on your team and their performance. This requires emotional intelligence (also known as EQ), which is the ability to understand and manage your own emotions, as well as recognise and influence the emotions of everyone around you. Although EQ has become a bit of a buzzword in the corporate world over the past two decades, that doesn't reduce its impact and importance when it comes to balanced leadership. EQ and balanced leadership are intertwined.

In Part One of this book, we lay out six leadership spectrums that relate to different styles of leadership, and we examine how these may be appropriate in different scenarios. It is not a definitive list of possible leadership spectrums, but it certainly touches upon many key dilemmas that organisations encounter and should therefore form a solid foundation to describe the challenges of balanced leadership. To achieve the best balance in any given circumstance, your starting point needs to be some self-awareness about where you naturally gravitate on each scale. Do you, for example, tend towards focusing on the big picture and neglect the detail? Or are you always supremely confident, never seeing the need for humility? Your natural approach may well not be appropriate in certain circumstances. To adjust this behaviour, in each case you need to understand which end of the scale you tend to gravitate towards. To help you in this endeavour, there are questions at the end of each chapter that will help you judge where you most naturally sit.

It is also worth noting that we all have some real blind spots when it comes to our working styles. These are things we think we are good at, when in reality we are actually quite poor at dealing with them. If we don't recognise and address these blind spots, it can severely impact our attempts at balance. If you want to do some preliminary work to look at where those blind spots are, I would point you in the direction of the Johari Window model, featured below in Figure 3. The Johari Window is a psychological tool, created by Joseph Luft and Harrington Ingham in 1955, and is designed to assist in the understanding of skills such as self-awareness, empathy, cooperation and group development.[1] The model works using four area quadrants, where everything you know about yourself, or are prepared to share, is part of your open arena. You can build trust by disclosing information to others or learning from others via the information they disclose about themselves. Anything that you don't know or recognise about yourself, but that others in your organisation know, is in your blind area. With some thought, as well as help and feedback from others, you

1 'Johari Window' (Wikipedia, n.d.), https://en.wikipedia.org/wiki/Johari_window.

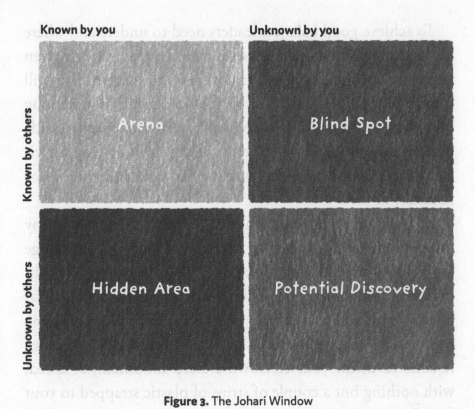

Figure 3. The Johari Window

can become more aware of some of your positive and negative tendencies. There's also a hidden area, where there are aspects about you and your life that you don't want others to know, as well as one for things that are unknown to you or anyone else. As you may expect, the balance between the four quadrants can change, but you do have influence over it. It is, for example, possible to expand your arena by asking those around you for feedback. The good bit about this is that when feedback is given honestly, it can reduce the size of your blind area. In other words, working with others is a good way to start when it comes to discovering the qualities that will help you move towards balance.

To achieve good balance, leaders need to understand where they naturally sit on each of the balance spectrums in any given situation and then they can choose how to behave. This will mean developing skills in all aspects of leadership. If something doesn't come naturally, a leader will need to build up that side of their armoury and be entirely willing to use the appropriate skill to the full when necessary, even when it doesn't come naturally at first.

I'll give you an extreme example (in every sense!), from my own experience, to show how difficult this can be. I'm a huge fan of professional skiing. One of my guilty pleasures is watching *Ski Sunday* on the BBC. I skied a bit myself while I was in the army and I was lucky enough to be selected for my regimental skiing team, so I know a little about what courage it takes to throw yourself down a steep mountain, at speed, with nothing but a couple of strips of plastic strapped to your feet. I'm an 'okay' skier, technique-wise, but nowhere near the league of the professionals when it comes to downhill racing. The biggest difference between us, though, is that I was never willing to push myself to the edge of control. Fast skiing is all about getting to the very knife edge of being completely out of control. If you can't do that, you won't get a look in. The people who win push themselves closer and closer to the line of completely wiping out – and indeed some do – but that's what it takes to win. They get the balance between skill, technique, experience and courage just right. The same goes for becoming an effective, balanced leader. Even if heading to the other side of the balance spectrum seems like a terrifying prospect, that is what needs to be done if you want to be the best.

Not everyone will manage it, but those who do will become outstanding leaders.

To be a truly balanced leader, we need to focus on developing the qualities we would rather ignore, or feel uncomfortable about developing, so we can introduce them when they are needed in a particular situation. To find the right balance, a leader needs to find a new way of acting. It can be a real test of true courage to take action appropriate for the situation.

Of course, simply exhorting leaders to keep trying to 'be nicer' or 'be more emphatic' in a given situation does not make it so. Plus, if it doesn't come naturally, it is difficult to be authentic when attempting an unfamiliar approach. No one likes dealing with someone whose behaviour seems forced. This is why Part Two of this book focuses on some of the skills balanced leaders need to perfect their approach, and there are a number of exercises to help you practise them. There will be a need for some degree of ongoing self-management, at least in the early days, but after a while these skills will begin to feel like second nature. It's useful to keep an eye on things, though. Balanced leaders should certainly keep checking their responses against the spectrums listed in Part One.

The challenge here is that it is not simply a question of mastering a range of skills to achieve balance. To be a balanced leader, you also need to judge *when* a particular skill is needed, and be prepared to change rapidly, again and again, each time according to the prevailing conditions. Some leaders instinctively seem to know when to switch between leadership styles, while others have to work harder on their judgement. This is why it is crucial for leaders to fully embrace what is going on around them. 'Reading the room' requires self-awareness, which is where EQ really comes into play. You cannot, for example, be empathetic to people unless you can understand their motivations and emotions. Leadership is, after all, fundamentally about the relationship between people. It's about the feeling that makes you want to go the extra mile for someone you work with. It is impossible to be empathetic with people, unless relationships have been built with them and the boss has taken the time to better understand what it is that makes them tick. What is it that's driving them?

Balanced leadership requires constant versatility. In the military there is a perfect phrase for this that describes what every new recruit learns from the get-go: 'adapt and overcome'. After months and years of training, the automatic response of anyone in the forces, to any problem they encounter, is to adapt to the new environment and overcome the challenges they face. The reason why this needs to be our instinctive reaction is obvious. As famously popularised through Charles Darwin's theory of natural selection, it is crucial for survival to quickly adapt to new environments in shifting circumstances. At the first sign of a new threat, operating procedures are swiftly tailored to the emerging situation.

While adaptability is ingrained in the military, and is a hugely useful, often life-saving skill, it does not come naturally to many people in business. Why? The answer can quite possibly be traced back to the very beginnings of our careers. In contrast to the versatile 'adapt and overcome' strategy that is drilled into military recruits, when people start corporate careers they are employed for a particular skill set, such as marketing, sales, technology or accounting. There is an implicit and in-built expectation that should circumstances change, someone else in the wider team will step in, leaving individuals to go on doing what they are doing according to their own specialism. As these individuals rise up through the hierarchy of the business and become more senior, all being well, the penny will drop that they now need to take charge of their own adaptation. It is no longer simply up to 'other people' in another room. However, this is not always the case. Certainly, this key business skill is rarely spoken about or part of the training and career development process. In fact, most leadership training modules are decidedly linear, rather like those in the leadership books mentioned earlier. They focus on the fact that if you do X, you will get Y. As a consequence, everyone learns to do X in response to a certain stimulus and Z in response to another stimulus. However, this way of working is massively limiting. If the context changes, as it so often does – and sometimes very quickly too – that way of working no longer applies. The carefully trained-in response is entirely redundant. To achieve balance, you cannot apply a linear model. What worked before in one situation will not necessarily translate to a new situation.

What makes this particularly tough is that the need to keep rebalancing is relentless. No leader can straighten everything up and then relax, job done. It is a constant juggling act. It puts me in mind of the epic naval movie *Master and Commander*, starring Russell Crowe as Captain Jack Aubery. Captain Aubery is ordered to hunt down and capture a powerful French vessel off the South American coast. He and the crew face a number of obstacles and, during a tense stand-off,

Aubery has to repeatedly switch between being an unyielding, decisive commander and a compassionate, understanding leader, all while maintaining the respect of his crew.

A balanced leader needs to constantly assess the situation and adapt accordingly. Perhaps a less combative way of looking at the process would be to liken it to a golfer choosing a golf club, using a calculated analysis of the challenge in question, with one eye on the end goal and making use of their acquired experience as to what is the best tool for the job. Is a small adjustment in play needed, or is an entirely new strategy required? Translate this to the workplace and if, say, there is an internal issue, the leader needs to judge whether all a team needs is a (metaphorical) warm hug, or whether an entirely new and visionary way of coaching is required in the light of a developing situation. Occasionally, of course, a team may require an (also metaphorical) kick in the bike shorts.

To properly adapt and overcome, and instinctively change when balance is required, you need to have a deep understanding of the *principles* of balance at all levels. Roderic has a good metaphor for this. He is, by his own admission, a poor cook. It's a product of being in the military in his formative years, where meals were all made for him. His disinterest in the process has endured in civilian life. He can, however, follow a recipe and make something that tastes sort of okay. That doesn't make him an expert, though. An expert chef is someone who understands the principles of taste on a foundational level. They could go into any kitchen, where the cupboards contain any assortment of ingredients, and make something that tastes amazing, because they understand the foundations of how taste works. They understand it on such a level that they can improvise, adjust themselves to the unfamiliar situation (a different kitchen) and still produce something outstanding. Expertise is having an understanding to such a level that you don't need to follow a set of ingredients to make something that tastes amazing.

In this book, instead of recipes, we are studying principles, and these principles are relevant to whatever situation you find yourself in. Understand the principles and learn the necessary skills, and you will be well on your way.

The whole purpose of this book is to help you to be adaptable to the context that you are facing. However, you can't continuously improve unless you are willing to change yourself. The two go hand in hand. You may be okay as you are, but you could be better. 'Adapt and overcome' is something we should all be practising, whatever our backgrounds. Adapting to a new set of circumstances, or a new context, is a conscious decision and is the foundation of balanced leadership.

PART ONE
THE SPECTRUMS OF LEADERSHIP

CHAPTER TWO

CENTRALISED _ DEVOLVED
CONTROL _ RESPONSIBILITY

There's a bit of a myth that surrounds the military, depicting it as all about command and control. Orders are ruthlessly barked out by officers, and their cowed reports respond and act without question, so the story goes. For the most extreme example, think of Gunnery Sergeant Hartman in the 1987 Stanley Kubrick film *Full Metal Jacket*. The reality is that there is a lot more empowerment down through the ranks than you might imagine.

Roderic's experience of his deployment to Afghanistan in 2007 is a perfect example of this nuance. A number of the Marines in his troop were less than 20 years old. Some were as young as 18. The youngsters had joined up straight out of school and only had a limited formal education. Being plunged into a brutal conflict like this is pretty intimidating for experienced soldiers and must have been especially tough on these raw recruits. Roderic was very aware that these young Marines were often initially hesitant to pull the trigger on their weapon. This was down to a mix of a natural nervousness about going into battle and fear over the repercussions should they make a bad judgement call. Roderic clearly had two choices about how to deal with the situation. He could follow in the footsteps of the overbearing Gunnery Sergeant Hartman and yell at everyone to get on with it, or he could find a better way of motivating his team in this dangerous environment, where any hesitation could be fatal.

Roderic thought back to his own first deployment, fresh out of training. Back in the UK, when he was first taught how to change a rifle magazine, he'd been shown a technique where he rapidly slipped the empty magazine into his combat jacket to speed up the changeover during a live-firing exercise. After numerous times doing just that, the system became second nature, which is obviously the point of military training exercises. However, one week into his deployment in Afghanistan, Roderic realised that the entire process had a fatal flaw. He and the rest of the troop were not wearing jackets in the stifling desert heat. Instead, they were wearing body armour, which is cut close to the body and is stiff and unyielding. Certainly, there is no space in which to slip a magazine. Two things became clear to Roderic in that moment. The first was that the people who had trained him in the art of securing magazines in jackets had most likely never been in a firefight where they had needed to change a magazine, and they definitely hadn't been in one in a very hot climate. The second was that Roderic had had to adapt his thinking to an entirely different theatre of operations. But, and this was key, he knew that his training had also empowered him to make decisions like this on the ground. He had been taught to think on his feet, adapt and find the best way to work under the new circumstances.

In the case of the young new Marines under his command, Roderic had to be sure that they felt empowered too and able to take responsibility for their own actions when they needed to pull the trigger. In reality, there was no other option: the troops were going to be spread out across the ground and needed to make their own decisions, often in a split second. Roderic could not be at all of their shoulders at every moment, yelling at them to react and pull the trigger. To help them get to a position where they were comfortable pulling the trigger under their own volition, Roderic reminded the Marines of the rules of engagement, which gave them a framework to show when it was the right time to pull the trigger. He also instilled in them the knowledge that the decision to fire had to be made very quickly. Finally, he let them know that if they made the decision to fire, he would back them 100%. While occasionally Roderic did need to resort to command and control, and shout to get the momentum going, this was not his dominant leadership style. On the whole, the most effective way to meet the objectives and keep everyone safe was to empower his troops and make them responsible for their own actions.

NO NEED TO SHOUT!

Frequently raised voices in an office is probably the most likely outward sign that a leader errs towards a command-and-control style of leadership. However, it is actually very rare for this physical manifestation of the leadership style to really be necessary. In fact, I can think of only four circumstances where it might be legitimate. The first is when the person in charge genuinely can't be heard because there is so much noise going on that in order to get the point across, they need to shout. During a firefight would be an example. Another would be when skippering a yacht, when the sound of the wind wailing and sails flapping can be hard to break through. There are not many corporate situations where people really can't be heard. Situation two would be another military scenario, where a commander needs to exert influence on their troops *right now* to impress upon them the urgency of the situation in the light of a looming potential danger. In this case, a bellowed order would be appropriate. The third scenario is similar and is when life is genuinely in danger; at that particular point, an urgent warning needs to be given. Again, neither scenario is common in the boardroom. Finally, a raised voice is occasionally used to motivate people and help them move towards a goal with more urgency, as in: 'Come on, let's go faster! Let's make this happen!' It's about geeing people up and getting them going. Overuse, or injudicious use, of such a technique may be exhausting for all concerned, though, and probably won't be that effective after a while.

As you can probably surmise, it is rare that the shouting style of command and control is ever needed in civilian or corporate life. Yet, most people will be familiar with leaders who like to yell and throw their weight about. One of the most well-known examples of this is Fred Goodwin, the former chief executive of Royal Bank of Scotland (RBS), who earned the nickname 'Fred the Shred' thanks to his habit of regularly 'shredding' people in front of colleagues if they earned his displeasure.[2] The practice of continually yelling and bawling at a team clearly sends things entirely out of balance, though. It's

---

2   Ian Fraser, *Shredded: Inside RBS, the Bank that Broke Britain* (New York: Birlinn, 2014).

a point very well demonstrated by the collapse of RBS, which had been put in such a vulnerable condition by a series of take-overs (which Fred the Shred had bulldozed through) that it came within hours of running out of cash in the 2008/9 global credit crisis and had to be rescued with a £45 billion bailout.

None of this is to say that a direct leadership style does not occasionally have some advantages. It can – just minus the shouting bit. Certainly, when a team is inexperienced, or unfamiliar with the duties they are required to do, the command-and-control leadership style can be useful. By passing on their knowledge and expertise via detailed instructions, the leader transfers their experience to each member of the team, helping them towards a positive outcome. Also, where a large number of people are involved in a task, when someone takes control, no one is left in any doubt about their part in delivering the project. A leader will deliver clear expectations to follow and goals to achieve, which can go a long way towards lowering stress levels among the team, who may be nervous about what might seem like an ambitious project.

Problems always occur when a boss takes the command-and-control style too far, loses their temper and starts raising their voice – or even shouting. It means they have lost control. If you want to lead well, you need to stay calm, allow the team space to think for themselves, and give the team genuine responsibility. Doing so accepts that they might make mistakes – and they may even fail – but they can learn from those lessons and next time they'll get it right. I have had experience of both extremes of leadership and can say right now that the more collegial approach is far, far more effective.

In 2019, I skippered a yacht in the Fastnet Race, a biennial offshore yacht race organised by the Royal Ocean Racing Club. Everybody on the crew knew someone else on the crew, but not everyone knew everyone else. It meant we were all quite likeminded souls. We were also asked to take along a representative of the owner of the boat for insurance purposes. As it happened, this person was a phenomenally experienced sailor, who had twice raced around the world as skipper. I quickly discovered during training that his leadership style and mine were 180 degrees different. At one point, we were working on perfecting our spinnaker drills. For those who are not familiar with yachts, the spinnaker is the large, usually highly colourful, sail that balloons out in front of a boat when it is deployed. It is quite a complicated sail to put up because there are a lot of ropes involved and you need to make sure everything is done properly, in the right order. If anything goes wrong and the sequence of events is broken, it can take at least 30 minutes to an hour to unravel the mistake before you start all over again. In a race situation, this is time you really don't have, so it is important the whole crew know exactly what to do. You want to get it right first time.

My approach to the complex spinnaker drills was to build up the team's skills nice and slowly, getting one bit right at a time before moving on to the next part of the process. Over time, as they became more familiar with what needed to be done, I intended to increase the pace, building up to race speed once everyone was comfortable. I wanted to be in a position where the team could work things out for themselves and problem solve if they needed to. Thus, as we practised the sequence, we agreed on a series of one-word commands, which they could easily interpret and implement without me having to step in and hold their hands every step of the way. I sensed straight away that the owner representative was impatient with this approach and was itching to get stuck in. When he did make a contribution, it was clear that he was very much the command-and-control type: step up, shout and keep shouting at everyone until they picked up the pace sufficiently. I explained as politely as I could that, to me, this was entirely the wrong approach. As soon as you begin shouting, you put people under pressure. When people are under pressure, they make mistakes and then, in this case, we'd need to spend up to an hour sorting out the mistake. It was far more effective to take the time now, spending a few extra minutes to get it right in the first place.

The two different leadership styles were put to the test during the race itself. I happened to be off watch in the cabin when the spinnaker needed to be raised. The other guy seized his moment, took control and put everyone under huge pressure to perform. Immediately. Just as I had predicted, a lot of the crew crumbled under the pressure and mistakes were made. That hour to unravel the mistakes was no longer theoretical – it was a reality, and right in the middle of the race too. When I learned what was happening, I returned to deck to calm things down, but by then the situation had progressed too far. The adrenaline was flowing and those mistakes had been made. It was a lesson learned the hard way. Empowering people to get on with it in a calm, measured manner is a better way to get things done.

THE ULTIMATE PARADOX

Getting the right balance between a controlling style of leadership that is not too pressured, and one that devolves responsibility to the team, is not easy – particularly for anyone new to leadership. Indeed, one of the most difficult challenges for anyone who has been promoted into a leadership role is shifting from *doing*, and being part of the team, to *leading*. In the army, it is often said that the hardest promotion of all is the one from private to lance corporal. Here, for the first time, a young person who has often lived with four others in a room, trained alongside them and relaxed together as friends, will find themselves as their boss. Do they carry on going out for a beer with everyone at the end of the week? Do they show that, underneath it all, they are still one of the team? Or, do they go to the other extreme and steer well clear of any sort of socialising and start throwing their weight around to show who is the boss? Many, many new leaders choose the former option. They doggedly insist on clinging to their previous role, partly because this is what they know best and what they've been rewarded for in the past. It's also partly fuelled by a fear of making mistakes. Either way, it is a really difficult transition for many people to make and it is not a situation that is unique to the armed forces either. All new leaders have to face a change in pace and circumstances.

The other scenario is where a new leader tries to operate at both extremes of the spectrum. I've seen plenty of situations where the person in charge is far too eager to not only control events but also to roll up their sleeves and get involved.

Frequently, this means shouldering time-consuming tasks that should really have been left to the people being paid to do them. Meanwhile, of course, there is the pressing issue of other complex leadership responsibilities that also need to be attended to. The leader's solution is to try to do everything. However, any leader who attempts to be all things to all people may well find themselves burning out quite quickly (as well as probably neglecting key tasks). Or, even if they are not quickly burnt out, they'll certainly be heading that way, since sticking to such a demanding routine will require a lot of early mornings and late nights. Stress levels will inevitably soar and the situation can even lead to health problems, both mental and physical. Whatever the outcome, it's not exactly conducive to clear-headed, measured leadership.

The urge to jump in and be in the thick of things presents leaders with the ultimate paradox. Leaders need to be on top of everything, but achieving this goal often means they need to be less involved, not more. When leaders are entirely focused on being in the thick of it, controlling every manoeuvre, they are *busy* but are they *productive*? Or, at least, are they productive in terms of their leadership position?

I know from personal experience that it is very difficult to get this balance right and distance yourself from some team tasks. While I have always tried to adhere to the very wise adage that you should seek not to do anything that could be done by someone else in the organisation who is paid less than you, I have not always succeeded. One of my earliest lessons in this respect occurred when I finished my training and got ready to lead my first platoon of soldiers. It was a big moment for me and I was really keen to get it right from the off. I wanted to show everyone what sort of leader I could be.

As luck would have it, the very last thing I did in training before departing for my new post was an exercise called Grim Reaper. The clue is very much in the title and it is justifiably well known as a tough training challenge. If I were to summarise it, I'd say it was an elaborate ten-day-long sleep-deprivation exercise. Normally, participants need a week to recover from Grim Reaper and even that is often not enough. Except, in my case, I came straight off the exercise and departed to my new posting.

I must have looked a bit of a sight when I arrived, because my new platoon sergeant took a sharp intake of breath when we met. He was a lovely guy called Frank McPhilips, but he'd been around the block for a while and knew complete exhaustion when he saw it. I tried to deflect attention from my somewhat depleted demeanour by asking Frank where the boys were and was informed that they were busy digging trenches.

'Great, no problem,' I said, summoning up my warmest smile from wherever it was hiding in the depths of my weary soul. 'I'll go and join them.'

In my mind, getting into the trench with the boys was the best and only way to make a great first impression and show that I was willing to get myself muddy and be part of the team.

Sergeant McPhilips was having none of it.

'No, sir,' he said, shaking his head emphatically. 'The boys are fine. They can dig trenches all day long. They won't like it, but they can get it done. You jumping in to help will make no difference. What we do need from you is to get some sleep.

We will need your brain in two days' time when we know the enemy will be kicking us.'

To emphasise the point, he refused point blank to even give me a shovel. I must have looked pretty bad!

As it turned out, Sergeant McPhilips was completely right. It went against my every instinct to go and lie down, but it was completely the right decision. I wanted to be in the trenches, but my strengths were much better deployed planning for the forthcoming battle and leading the execution of it. After some rest, I met the platoon, who weren't in the least bit bothered that I had not spent time digging with them. They were, however, delighted when I led them through the subsequent battle, where everything went perfectly.

OFTEN IT IS BETTER TO STEP BACK – BUT NOT TOO FAR

I learned an interesting lesson from the Grim Reaper scenario. Your mind can and will play tricks on you. It's easy to get swayed by what you *think* you *should* do, or by what you've been trained to do, or even by external influences (i.e. what others think you should do). When it comes to leadership, though, you need to step back and do what you are best at (and give yourself the space to be firing on all cylinders when you are needed). It also helps to listen to those around you. Sergeant McPhilips may have been lower in rank than me, but he had ten more years of experience under his belt. His assessment of the situation was spot on. Devolving responsibility is not a sign of weakness: it is a sign of a strong leader.

It's quite useful to examine some of the other most common reasons behind why some leaders are too controlling and reluctant to leave their reports to get on with things. One of the most frequent (and possibly the most frustrating for the rest of the team) is where a leader thinks they can do a better job themselves. We all recognise this scenario: *it will take hours to explain what I want everyone to do, so I will be better off doing it myself.* There's so much wrong with this assumption. For a start, even if this is true the first time, if you let the team get on with the task, it won't be the case in the weeks and months to come. Perhaps more concerningly, this attitude means that the person in charge has no trust or faith in the abilities of their team, which is pretty demotivating for all involved. It also speaks volumes about the boss's confidence in their own skills – I don't mean because they think they are the best qualified in the room, but because they don't have the confidence to give up the position of always being the go-to person. They just can't get into the mindset that, actually, everyone wants to do good work and be successful.

Ironically, in some ways, a more controlling leadership style is actually the *easier* option for the leader themselves. The command-and-control approach of telling others what to do and then expecting it to happen is more simplistic. There is no real training required for this leadership style, or motivational techniques behind it to master in order to rally the troops. It's as simple as: *tell them what to do, how they should do it and how soon the job needs to be done.* End of. I'll add the caveat that there are the odd occasions when this somewhat blunt-instrument style of approach can work and even be motivational in itself. If, say, a team has experienced poor leadership in the past, or become disillusioned for whatever reason, a leader who doesn't pontificate could be the catalyst they need. At the very least, they will understand very clearly that if they fail to complete an assignment their position could be in jeopardy. It is not perhaps the most sophisticated way to get people on side, but it gets the job done, in all senses of the phrase. Overall, though, it's not an ideal long-term solution to leading a team.

It can be quite frustrating to work for a leader who insists on retaining *full* control in all circumstances. Yes, they do delegate, but only within very tightly defined parameters. They will initiate a project, define tasks, allocate responsibilities, and set deadlines, rules and boundaries. Direct reports are not invited to offer any alternative suggestions or give feedback on the feasibility of getting the job done in this way. They are left to get on with achieving the closely defined goals, with their performance subsequently judged on how well they achieved (or didn't achieve) their assigned tasks. Perhaps not surprisingly, leaders like this quickly gain a reputation of not listening. What happens then? Well, no one tells you anything, which is a dangerous position to be in.

While some teams may thrive with a highly directive leader, most will not. Certainly, any business that relies on any degree of creativity will struggle. People are, after all, being paid to come up with innovative solutions. It's not easy to do this against a highly prescriptive backdrop. Also, when it is impossible to take the initiative, there is a lack of ownership of key tasks, which is demoralising and unsatisfying for everyone involved.

I should also add here that delegating tasks and allowing room to make mistakes is not the same thing as completely devolving *all* responsibility. Yes, the person in charge has made the conscious decision to divide up the responsibilities, but they are still ultimately answerable for everything that happens in the organisation. It is entirely reasonable, therefore, that every now and again they will ask people: how is it going? What is the status of that project? Direct reports shouldn't see this as an affront to their independence.

Again, this is not an easy balance to achieve. It needs to be built into the culture of an organisation. People need to accept that while they've been empowered to do tasks, they will still be subject to some scrutiny, at least now and again. I worked with one professional services group where tremendous steps had been taken in the direction of delegating work to senior managers. The leader had made a great play of the fact he was empowering his team and giving them more autonomy, which was not just great for the business but also a real opportunity for the manager's career development. One of the beneficiaries of the new regime was the head of one of the company's divisions, who was put in charge of the company's annual sales conference. It was a tough challenge, involving coordinating speakers and delegates from all over the world, but this executive was delighted. It was something that stretched her skills and introduced her to a whole new environment. She set to work with great enthusiasm.

I was a little surprised when the executive approached me

a few weeks before the global event. Gone was the look of engagement and satisfaction. It had been replaced by a look of nothing short of deep anger.

'So much for empowerment,' she fumed. 'That's all gone out of the window.'

It transpired that the boss of the organisation had approached her a few hours earlier and asked for a rundown of the plans for the international conference. He was keen to receive a round-up of projected attendance, details of the speakers, and whether or not the project was on budget.

To me, this was not an unreasonable request and I told the executive just that. Anyone who is in charge of an organisation needs to retain control and understanding of all aspects of the operation, regardless of whether they are involved in the day-to-day management of individual piece. The boss had left the executive to get on with it – empowered her to be in sole charge of a crucial event – and was simply checking up a few days before so he could feel comfortable it would go as expected. Once the executive saw the situation from this viewpoint, she accepted the point. (And, as it turned out, the conference was a huge success.)

Overall, leadership success is a long-term journey and leaders need to take their teams with them. We need to accept that talent is not innate. It is not something we are born with. Our skills are something that we pick up and get better at with practice, and that means, crucially, learning from mistakes.

Command-and-control leaders rob people of the opportunity to make mistakes within a safe environment and never create an opportunity for individuals to learn. It takes a really confident leader to be comfortable with that and to devolve responsibility to the team. It is, however, a mark of a forward-looking, balanced organisation when leaders are willing to create the space for others to take risks and learn from them.

QUESTIONS

To help judge your natural inclination on a scale between centralised control and delegation *see* Table 1. Decide where you sit on each spectrum, where 1 means you strongly agree with the first statement, 2 means you somewhat agree with the first statement, 3 means you agree with each statement about equally, 4 means you somewhat agree with the second statement and 5 means you strongly agree with the second statement. There are no wrong answers – this is simply a guide to help you reflect and perhaps adjust where required.

	1	2	3	4	5	
I love being in control		2	3	4	5	I am comfortable not being in control
I find it difficult to delegate	1	2	3	4	5	I will always seek to delegate where appropriate
I have been accused of 'getting into the detail', e.g. Always checks the work of team members	1	2	3	4	5	I have never been accused of 'getting into the detail' e.g. Rarely checks the work of team members
I expect team members to follow the steps in line with their instructions	1	2	3	4	5	I am happy for team members to 'do it their way'
I value speed of decision-making over having a broad range of perspectives	1	2	3	4	5	I value a broad range of perspectives over speed of decision-making
I should not have to take responsibility for the mistakes of my team members	1	2	3	4	5	I am comfortable taking responsibility for the mistakes of my team members
I believe the role of the leader is to retain control	1	2	3	4	5	I believe the role of the leader is to share control
I sometimes clash with my team because they want greater freedom and responsibility	1	2	3	4	5	I sometimes clash with my team because they want greater support and guidance

Table 1. Centralised Control and Devolved Responsibility

CHAPTER THREE

CONFIDENCE — HUMILITY

When we hear the word 'leader', most of us will conjure up a vision of a strong-minded individual who is always courageous and bold enough to be in the front line of any situation. There's a clear link in perception between leadership and power. Whenever anyone is cast in a leadership position, there is an unspoken pressure to shoulder any difficulties, brushing them off as mere inconveniences, even if they are anything but. Perhaps, though, the description that unifies the vision of leadership most of all is 'confidence'.

It is absolutely true that confidence is a crucial trait in any leader. It is the quality that ensures that the person in charge is willing to stick their neck out and champion projects that others might feel are too risky or too much bother. By the same token, if a project doesn't appear to be going the way it was anticipated, a confident leader will be courageous about saying, 'This isn't working – let's ditch it and try something else.' They'll recognise the issues more quickly than others, and be willing to pull the plug regardless of the optics. Anyone who works with a highly confident leader will most likely say that they exude energy and enthusiasm. It's infectious too. Reports expect to be challenged and there is an understanding that this type of leader will be keen to motivate others to follow up on tough tasks. Their style is definitely more pull than push. When it comes to championing the efforts of their team, a confident leader is always out in front.

But is confidence the only quality that leaders require to inspire the people around them to strive harder and do better? There is a strong argument that they need to balance all this confidence with a little humility too.

HUMILITY DOES NOT EQUAL WEAKNESS

At face value, humility is a tough one to pull off for any leader, particularly someone who is new to the top job and who is very keen to be *seen* as being in charge. Few people really expect a leader to be self-effacing or humble. It feels too closely linked with subservience, or even weakness. Certainly, it simply doesn't fit the accepted powerful narrative of a visionary, charismatic leader. Perhaps, though, it is just the word 'humility' that puts us off. Throw away your preconceptions for a moment and let's drill down into what humility really means.

People who display this trait are known to be good listeners. They're great at teamwork too, because they do their utmost to involve everyone and really focus on their strengths. They don't feel threatened if someone is better at an element of a task than they are: that's cool. It gets the job done in the best possible way. Other traits associated with humility are a willingness to solicit and listen to feedback and a higher level of engagement. Say it like this, and humility doesn't sound like such a bad thing, right?

There's more too. Another of the interesting things about

humility (which also has a bearing on the subject of the previous chapter: centralised control–devolved responsibility) is that leaders with this trait are more willing to accept that they are not always the smartest person in the room. Thus, they encourage people to speak up, regardless of their position in the company. Their view is that everyone – from a production-line employee to a board-level executive – has a pertinent view, so it makes sense to hear it. If they harness these people's input, it may well be to the betterment of the entire business. As Steve Jobs once said, 'It doesn't make sense to hire smart people and tell them what to do; we hire smart people so they can tell us what to do.'[3]

To be fair, not everyone is instantly dismissive of the quality of humility. In the ground-breaking book *Good to Great* by Jim Collins, the author found that two crucial traits of successful chief executives, which helped their companies to transition from average to superior market performance, were humility and a steadfast will to advance the cause of the whole organisation.[4] Humble leaders know how to get the best out of everyone.

Ah, you may be saying, but what about the perception of weakness? If the rest of the team thinks I am too timid or too easily swayed, won't they underestimate me? Or, worse still, ignore me? The answer is no. As well as the tendencies above, humility is closely linked with a number of very positive traits,

---

3   Quoted in Victor Lipman, 'The best sentence I ever read about managing talent' (*Forbes*, 25 September 2018), https://www.forbes.com/sites/victorlipman/2018/09/25/the-best-sentence-i-ever-read-about-managing-talent.
4   Jim Collins, *Good to Great: Why Some Companies Make the Leap... and Others Don't* (London: Random House Business, 2001).

such as sincerity, modesty, fairness, truthfulness and authenticity (the last of which I believe is one of the most important leadership qualities of all). This authentic style of leadership has been shown to be one of the most powerful styles when it comes to employee satisfaction, commitment and workplace happiness.[5]

I believe authenticity is key to unlocking the right balance between super-confidence at one end and a little bit of humility at the other, because both qualities are essential to balanced leadership. One of the most important components of authenticity is a healthy dose of self-awareness. This doesn't mean in the arrogant sense of 'look at me, I'm a great leader'. It refers to a leader's understanding of their strengths *and* weaknesses.

There is no game-playing here, just a genuine willingness to hear the views of others and feel empathy for their point of view. This also means that the authentic leader is very open to frank discussions about performance. An authentic leader will encourage feedback in a bid to understand why something didn't work as well as hoped. They'll also be confident enough to hear a number of viewpoints before choosing a plan of action. Overall, an authentic leader encourages a culture of open and honest debate. They demand that people properly execute the tasks they are entrusted with, but are open to ideas on new approaches.

5 Susan M. Jensen and Fred Luthans, 'Entrepreneurs as authentic leaders: Impact on employees' attitudes', *Leading & Organizational Development Journal*, vol. 27, no. 8 (2006), pp. 646–666; Sandra Penger and Matej Černe, 'Authentic leadership, employees' job satisfaction, and work engagement: A hierarchical linear modelling approach', *Economic Research*, vol. 27, no. 1, pp. 508–526.

CONFIDENCE IS GOOD, BUT NOT WHEN IT SPILLS OVER INTO ARROGANCE

Most people have worked with a leader who is absolutely 100% certain of their own power and influence. This type of leader is so supremely arrogant, they've become utterly consumed with an unhealthy sense of their own importance. The signs are pretty obvious. These are the leaders who are more interested in looking for ways for the team to serve *them*, rather than

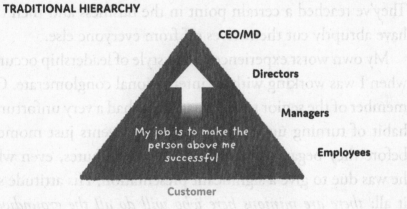

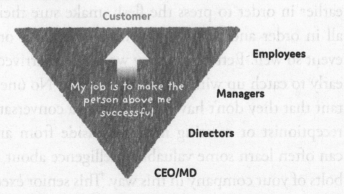

Figure 4. Traditional hierarchy versus serve-to-lead approach

the other way around. (Figure 4 is a useful illustration of the 'serve-to-lead' approach versus the traditional hierarchy.) They're focused on their personal goals and achievements, with no real interest in how the organisation as a whole is doing. If anything doesn't go to plan, they shy away from owning poor results, either spinning them to be something quite different or placing the blame firmly on the team. You can forget about an open-door policy too. Arrogant leaders have an invitation-only policy when it comes to their inner sanctum. They've reached a certain point in the business and then they have abruptly cut themselves off from everyone else.

My own worst experience of this style of leadership occurred when I was working with an international conglomerate. One member of the senior team in particular had a very unfortunate habit of turning up to major company events just moments before they began – I mean only a few minutes, even when he was due to give a significant presentation. His attitude said it all: *there are minions here who will do all the groundwork; all I need to do is walk in there and deliver my speech.* Even a super-confident leader would have arrived at least 10 minutes earlier in order to press the flesh, make sure their slides were all in order and thank everyone involved for organising the event so well. Better still, they would have arrived 30 minutes early to catch up with everyone properly. No one is so important that they don't have time to have a conversation with the receptionist or catering manager. Aside from anything, you can often learn some valuable intelligence about the nuts and bolts of your company in this way. This senior executive was so arrogant he really didn't feel it necessary to give anyone even a few seconds of his time. It did not go unnoticed at any level in the organisation – and rightly so.

PICK YOUR MOMENT

The clear message when it comes to confidence and humility is this: there is a balance to be had and all leaders should avoid going to one extreme (or far beyond it) and staying there. The art is in learning when to be super-confident and when a little humility would go a long way. Think about the variables surrounding a significant decision about the way forward for the organisation:

- Do you make and vocalise a decision and then tell everyone to get on with it – no further debate required – because we are going this way?

  or

- Do you open the decision up to discussion and debate, and empower team members to say what they really think?

In truth, you need to make these calls on a situation-by-situation basis and, as I discovered, this is a balance that is definitely learned through experience. Let me tell you about an experience I had while sailing that shows how I learned this.

On this occasion, the yacht I was skippering was sailing around the Mull of Kintyre when the weather turned against us. The added peril in this situation is that it is a tough stretch of water even in calm weather. There are two big bodies of water either side of the peninsula and, when the tide turns, an incredibly strong current flies around the headland in both directions. If the wind is going in the wrong direction *and* the weather is bad, you're in a lot of trouble. Sure enough, we were caught in this awful situation. To make matters even worse for us, we hadn't given the overfalls (shallower water that creates very large and unpredictable waves in certain states of tide and wind) a wide enough berth, making a bad situation pretty drastic indeed.

I was in the unenviable position of feeling pretty seasick, but I also had a real sense of panic to add to my heady mix of emotions. I was doing my utmost not to show any discomfort, and my oft-used mantra of *keep it together* didn't seem to be having a positive effect, although I will admit it was interspersed with some stronger language. Added to that, there was a real sense that I had led us into this potential disaster. If anything terrible happened, which at the time seemed fairly certain to be the case, it was 100% on me.

We did, somehow, get through it. Afterwards, when we got back to the shore and everyone had recovered their wits and dried out, I was the first to admit I had got it wrong. I didn't wait for the 'Were you scared, skipper?' discussion. I immediately shifted the balance from appearing supremely confident to showing humility and came right out and admitted it to the crew. I told them that my legs had been shaking and there were moments when I had genuinely thought we were goners. Why did I say this only after we got to shore? It was unfeasible that I could have done so out on the water. It wasn't just that the crew would barely have heard me over the crashing of wild wind and waves. It was that I needed to be seen as supremely confident. *We are going to get through this.*

It's all fine. Follow me. After all, we had no choice but to sail on through it. However, once we were safe, I thought it was important to shift the balance and show some humility at the earliest opportunity.

That was an important part of how we reflected on the event. I needed to say, 'Guys, I probably got that a bit wrong.' Everyone knew that was the case, but I had to own it. If I had just breezed through it, move-on-nothing-to-see-here style, how could I ever have expected them to trust me again? It was crucial for team adhesion that I owned the mistake. I don't know it all and, now and again, I will make mistakes, although I won't make that one again!

I believe the lesson here was to pick your moment. When you are in charge, there is a time to be super-confident and lead the way, and there is a time to put your hands up and say you didn't get it completely right. Don't fail at either.

Interestingly, I told this story at a conference in the Middle East and one of the delegates became very animated in her response. Why, she wanted to know, was I so prepared to admit my mistakes? And so quickly too! Surely a leader should be the most experienced person in the room and should project this fact at every given opportunity.

This is quite an interesting viewpoint and, I think, quite integral to the balancing act between confidence and humility. As it happened, I was not the most experienced sailor on that particular yacht when we tried to sail around the Mull of Kintyre. That accolade went to another member of the crew, who had many more miles under his belt. Yet, while he was the most experienced sailor, he was probably the least appropriate skipper. By a long way. By his own admission. He didn't have the leadership skills or the desire to step up to the position. Thus, I deferred to him on certain matters but used my own leadership skills to direct the crew and make the required decisions. You could, quite validly, argue that we didn't get it right – but the important point here was that I led by example and gave the crew confidence. They followed my lead and we sailed out of there. I was self-assured when I needed to be and humble when the immediate danger was over. Frankly, becoming distracted by having to create an aura of being the most experienced, powerful leader couldn't have been further from my mind. As we've already discussed here, people get far too carried away with how a leader should be *seen*. It's completely unnecessary and disrupts the smooth flow in the required shift in balance between confidence and humility.

There is a great Sigmund Freud saying that sums this up perfectly. He said that we leak the truth.[6] We can all *act* at being the great, powerful leader, or a man or woman of the people, but we can only ever manage it for short periods of time if it is not really who we are. It won't be long before we cut back to being our true selves. As all leaders know only too well, there are occasions when you need to 'fake it until you make it'. Just as I did, you will have to project a high state of confidence when you feel anything but. However, this cannot be a permanent state of affairs. It's crucial to snap back to being your authentic self as soon as you can. Fortunately for

6 'He that has eyes to see and ears to hear may convince himself that no mortal can keep a secret. If his lips are silent, he chatters with his fingertips; betrayal oozes out of him at every pore.' Sigmund Freud, quoted in 'Freud in quotes' (Freud Museum London, 2019), https://www.freud.org.uk/2019/04/30/freud-in-quotes.

me, I only had to pretend to be super-confident on that yacht for a hair-raising hour or so. As soon as we were back safely, I reverted to being me and shared my true feelings with my crew. They appreciated that authenticity and it enhanced our already strong bond. I think if I had continued swaggering it out, or even left it too long before explaining my true feelings, they would have lost a lot of respect for me.

QUESTIONS

To help judge your natural inclination on a scale between centralised control and delegation *see* Table 2 on the following page. Decide where you sit on each spectrum, where 1 means you strongly agree with the first statement, 2 means you somewhat agree with the first statement, 3 means you agree with each statement about equally, 4 means you somewhat agree with the second statement and 5 means you strongly agree with the second statement. There are no wrong answers – this is simply a guide to help you reflect and perhaps adjust where required.

	1	2	3	4	5	
I have complete faith in my abilities	1	2	3	4	5	I am unsure of my abilities from time to time
I am not comfortable admitting when I have made mistakes	1	2	3	4	5	I am comfortable admitting when I have made mistakes
I believe I am amongst the top of my peer group in my field	1	2	3	4	5	I don't believe that I amongst the top of my peer group
Team members don't very often challenge my point of view/ideas/direction	1	2	3	4	5	Team members often challenge my point of view/ideas/direction
I believe that my team are here to help me	1	2	3	4	5	I believe my role is to help my team
I don't value humility in others	1	2	3	4	5	I value humility in others
I always share my ideas first	1	2	3	4	5	I always share my ideas last

Table 2. Confidence and Humility

CHAPTER FOUR
CHALLENGING — SUPPORTIVE

There has never been a successful leader who has simply bumped along, seeing how things go and doing their best not to rock the boat too much. Sooner or later, the person at the top of an organisation needs to say: *this is not working – we need to do it like this now. Follow me.*

But, can people work in a highly challenging atmosphere 24/7, every week of the year? Can everyone on the team withstand a daily exhortation to test the unproven or dive deep into the unknown? *Let's go higher and faster – come on!* The answer has to be an emphatic *no.* Constant challenge would be exhausting and most likely hugely counterproductive. Team members would inevitably drop off, demoralised and worn out. No organisation can sustain this work rate indefinitely. Indeed, often, when things need to get done, it is more prudent for a leader to slow the pace down and pause to show their support and appreciation. Challenge needs to be offset by a firm foundation of support to be sustainable.

All leaders need people around them to help them achieve their goals, which means getting them to follow. The only way to achieve this is to find the winning mix of challenge *and* support to get the best out of a team. As Jack Welch, the former chief executive of General Electric, once said: 'Before you are a leader, success is all about growing yourself. When you become a leader, success is all about growing others.'[7] Achieving the right balance is never easy, though. This is, in part, because the amount of challenge or support required to get the desired effect can vary from individual to individual and from circumstance to circumstance. There is a large number of variables to understand and many judgement calls to be made.

THE ART OF CHALLENGE

Before we get to the most appropriate moments to deploy either challenge or support, let's begin by examining the two extremes so we can understand them better. We'll kick off with the challenging leader. The ability to challenge the status quo is the quality that is most frequently associated with leadership. Here, a leader is constantly focused on the best way to adapt and change an organisation to keep forward momentum. Their goal is to confront any stale thinking head on and ensure the business doesn't stagnate. They don't have to wait to intervene when things are 'broken' and need fixing, either. Challenging behaviour should never be wholly reactive. Challenging leaders need to be forward thinking enough to battle the status quo well ahead of the curve. The culture they create never accepts that the bare minimum is good enough. It is one where new perspectives are encouraged and there is a constant appetite for positive change.

I once had an illuminating conversation with someone who worked for the electronics and entertainment giant Apple. This

7   Jack Welch, Winning (New York: Harper Business, 2005).

business's meteoric rise is predicated on challenging norms and continuous improvement. After incorporating a camera into the iPhone, they didn't just clap each other on the back for a job well done before moving on to focus on what other features or widgets they could add next. No, the Apple team kept going back to the camera to see whether they could make it a bit better. The goal was to get it to the stage where it took better photos than a professional, stand-alone camera and then became even better than that. Apple's bosses were never willing to say, 'That will do – it is good enough.' They kept challenging the team to come up with something even better.

It's not just the 'big' stuff that catches the attention of Apple leadership and has them getting their team to revisit their designs over and over again. My Apple contact told me about an extremely lengthy search that was conducted to find the exact right paper to wrap around the box the iPhone comes in. Yes: the box. That thing that gets thrown away or shoved in a cupboard once the newly acquired phone has been removed. Apple's leadership understood that the experience of buying an iPhone is hugely important to the brand's fans. There is even a trend of filming the grand opening – or 'unboxing', as it is known – of a new phone and posting it online. Therefore, everything about the iPhone box needed to be perfect. More than perfect, in fact. Thus, Apple devoted intense scrutiny to the paper that was wrapped around the box. How could it be made better? The challenge laid down to the Apple design team was that the wrapping had to be thick enough that it didn't simply slip off yet lightweight enough that it was satisfying to unwrap, and very pleasing to the touch. It had to be easy to open, but not so easy that the process would be rushed and fail to live up to the anticipation. Oh, and the material used also had to fit in with Apple's environmental strategy, which dictates a shift to more recyclable and reusable content. It might not sound like a tall order seeing it written down here but, apparently, the search for the perfect wrapper entailed literally hundreds of different alternatives being tried. All that for the paper on the packaging. Can you imagine how many versions of the camera they tried?

The bulk of the responsibility for continuous improvement is, of course, ultimately in the hands of the team. They are, after all, the main custodians of that status quo and the ability to improve on it. Companies are the sum total of the parts of the people who work there. It is, therefore, a leader's role to push the team out of their comfort zone and challenge their thinking. Remaining with Apple for the moment, founder Steve Jobs had many techniques to keep his team on their toes. In one, he used to regularly demand that team members *defended* their ideas to their colleagues.[8] In his view, this sort of intense questioning ensured that ideas were properly thought through and had an entirely solid foundation. Time was therefore not wasted on poorly conceived, unjustified ideas and could, instead, be used to focus on concepts deemed to be workable. Jobs was notorious for giving his team a particularly hard time but the principle of challenge here is a good one. No one wants a team where everyone sticks to their guns, come what may, even when new information comes to light

---

8 Walter Isaacson, *Steve Jobs* (London: Little, Brown, 2011).

that shows their initial understanding is no longer as relevant. While changing one's mind is often seen as a sign of weakness – particularly in the political arena, where the media is quick to point the finger about U-turns – it is actually a sign of incredible strength. The concept of 'strong views, loosely held', where someone has strong opinions but is open to changing their mind if they are shown they have made a wrong assumption, is very compelling.

There are times when too much challenge can be, well, too much – certainly if it is not couched in the right terms. Done badly, it can seem like micro-management or, even more worryingly, like a bit of a power trip by the leader. Either way, perpetual challenge will become really, really difficult for everyone on the team. People will dread meetings because they know that each meeting will descend into a fight within minutes. The boss will demand, 'Do you really think that is the right response to this goal?' Or, 'Why have you not tried X?' Or, 'Have you been in touch with Y? She managed a similar situation with ease, just a few months ago.' Being seen as someone who constantly challenges every decision, however insignificant, is a good way to ensure some serious pushback from the team.

The way that challenges are perceived by the team has a lot to do with the culture at individual companies. If there is an atmosphere where rigorous debate is always welcomed, then it is much easier for a leader to probe the effectiveness of decisions being taken by offering an alternative view (as long as they are not doing so with every single decision). It also helps a lot if a challenging leader is always highly visible and approachable throughout the lifetime of a project. There's nothing that is destined to put people's backs up more than someone who has had no involvement whatsoever in something until the moment when they sweep in and question everything that's been done to date. In this instance, however carefully the challenge is couched, it will always seem an inappropriate response.

The pressure to 'over-challenge' can often stem from the need to show continuous growth. Yet, don't be surprised if a team baulks at constant demands to push up profits whatever it takes. Such edicts can become extremely demoralising and, ironically, produce the opposite effect. I once advised a UK-based conglomerate with a small satellite production facility in the US. The organisation had recently introduced a new strategy and it was all about growth, growth, growth. I had been brought in to explain the goals that had been set to the team in the American office. At that time, the US operation was staffed by about 30 people. When I arrived, I could see straight away that it was a very close-knit, dynamic team. They'd worked together to build the US division organically and were rightly very proud of their achievements. After I had outlined the new growth strategy, the reception was very positive.

'Fantastic! We've got this!' they said.

It was clear they thrived on a challenge. I had to step in and tell them to put the brakes on for a moment, though.

'I love the fact that you're so enthusiastic, but let's just look at this more deeply for a moment,' I said. 'These developments will see demand rise and more products going off the shelves.

You will need to ramp up production and may even need to develop new products. It's quite likely that you will need to take on new people – a lot of new people – and then move to new premises.

'How do you feel about that? You are clearly a very tight team.'

This really gave them pause for thought. After their enthusiastic response to the challenge of the expansion, they became very reflective. They enjoyed the current dynamic. They'd come to understand each other so well that they could anticipate one another's moves. They each knew that they could rely on the support of the others. They enjoyed the fact that they were small and nimble and could turn orders around in hours, something that would not be possible with a larger production facility. All of a sudden, the challenge of the relentless quest for growth didn't look as attractive. In fact, it seemed the very antithesis of the innovation and entrepreneurship that they valued so highly. Following this, they did, indeed, embrace change, but they did it with their eyes open. As a result they were able to ensure that while they grew in number and embraced new ways of working, they also retained the best of their original culture.

None of this is to say that growth is not good. Of course it is, and of course leaders should challenge their teams to keep delivering. However, things need to change and evolve. Yes, encourage the team to keep reaching for the stars, but recognise that they need more than instructions from the top to keep on getting bigger and bigger. They need to be shown why it matters and what it means to them. This requires encouragement and an environment of open and honest collaboration, which is at the other end of the challenging–supportive spectrum.

SUPPORTIVE LEADERSHIP

A culture of support is quite different from one of challenge. A supportive leader is much less likely to sweep in, make a demand and then move on. They make their presence known, checking in often and making sure that everyone is aware that they're around if required. As well as being more visible, the supportive leader encourages everyone to participate in decisions and is willing to coach where necessary. This more people-orientated, supportive leadership style has numerous advantages. It builds strong relationships with everyone on the team, which is motivating and keeps people focused. Individuals are less likely to be defensive or feel under pressure because they are not struggling under the weight of endless critical scrutiny. They don't feel over-managed either. This all helps towards creating an environment where everyone feels more engaged in the day-to-day work as well as in the long-term vision of the company. Ultimately, if people feel that they are heard, they enjoy what they do more and, ultimately, will do a better job.

There can, however, be disadvantages to the supportive leadership style if it is over done. If it goes too far, and the boss is constantly on the ground helping and steering everyone, there is a possibility that they will be seen as a bit too much of a soft touch. Indeed, there is an element where, the closer the lines are between the team and its leadership, the more those lines are blurred. A leader who is viewed as a friend, or on an equal footing, will find it difficult when they need to have a challenging conversation with one of their team members or hold them accountable for not meeting an achievable goal. These very close relationships also make it very difficult for the boss to move someone on who consistently underperforms. The result? Poor performers can be kept in place for far longer than is necessary.

Something that is often discussed in the context of supportive leadership is employee engagement, which is covered in Part Two. However, it will be useful to briefly address it here, since I feel there are, occasionally, times when this trend pushes the balance too far in the direction of support.

Let's start with a bit of background. In recent years, employee engagement has become a real battleground for competitive advantage. The idea behind it is that it should not simply be left to one person (the leader) to shoulder the entire burden, make every decision, constantly challenge and command every action. Instead, the person at the top should empower the team so that everyone is a player, rather than a spectator who is being bossed around and told what to do.

The main argument in favour of this infinitely more nurturing and supportive style of leadership is that many heads are greater than one. Colleagues are willing to speak truth to power and, since they are fully involved in the day-to-day running of the business, this provides invaluable intelligence. Those in favour of this style argue that the arrangement completely does away with the 'them and us' challenging style of leadership, which they say can lead to a destructive sort of disengagement. Disengaged employees generally fall into two camps. In the first, individuals are unhappy with their lot, but, worse still, are actively unhappy. They won't be interested in solving problems or stretching themselves. If they are customer facing, they may project this dissatisfaction to a wider world, which is troubling, and, even if they are not, they may take up a disproportionate amount of their line manager's time. The second group of the disengaged is equally concerning. These are the people who are fed up but who do just about enough to get by and keep their jobs. It's hardly dynamic behaviour and certainly not good for the prospects of

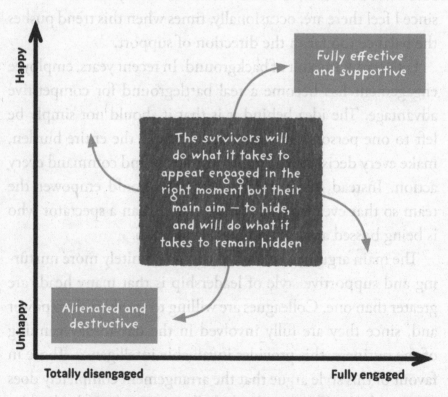

Figure 5. The spectrum of employee engagement

any organisation. The first group might be called 'alienated' and the second group 'survivors'. Figure 5 shows the range of behaviours that differentiate the alienated and the survivors.

There are ample signs that having a more engaged workforce does make sound commercial sense. Gallup, which has been measuring employee engagement for many years, says that organisations with an engaged workforce report better customer engagement, higher productivity, better employee retention, fewer accidents and 21% higher profitability.[9] It's pretty hard to argue with that. Yet, while it is absolutely clear that there are defined competitive advantages to improved employee engagement and that these definitely require a highly supportive leadership, I am wary that sometimes the pendulum swings too far towards this end of the spectrum and then remains there without question.

I once worked with a very interesting creative business that had, at one stage, won all sorts of 'best place to work in' types of award. I was called in because the gongs had disappeared. The question I was tasked with answering was: why weren't the team engaged any more? What had changed? The answer, as it turned out, was quite straightforward. The company had grown substantially since the early days, thanks in part to its highly enjoyable, supportive and inclusive culture. Everyone had had a lot of fun and they'd achieved some great stuff. Now, though, it had become a completely different organisation. The number of employees had swelled to 300 or so. Before, when there had been less than 30 people on the team, everyone had

---

9   Jim Harter, 'Employee engagement on the rise in the US' (Gallup, 26 August 2018), https://news.gallup.com/poll/241649/employee-engagement-rise.aspx.

known everyone else. It had been easy to keep up the buzzy culture and give individuals any support they required. Once the company had grown to more than ten times its original size, there was inevitably more process involved. Looking at this situation in terms of 'interaction ratios', as shown in Figure 6, if there are 30 people in an organisation, the interaction

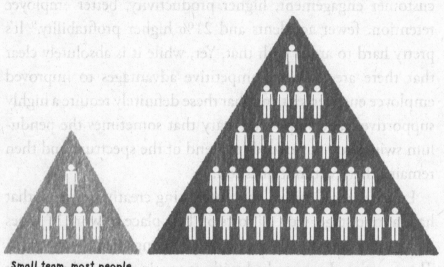

THE DIFFERENCE BETWEEN BIG AND SMALL COMPANIES

Small team, most people know each other. Trust is easier to generate. High interaction ratios.

Large organisation, few people know each other. Trust is harder to generate. Low interaction ratios.

Figure 6. Interaction ratios

ratios are high, but move to ten times that figure and the ratios drop dramatically. Silos emerge because people can only ever manage so many relationships. Think about it as the difference between a dinner party and a wedding.

In the case of this creative business, and others that expand and find themselves in this situation, leadership has to become more challenging to keep things on track. Things are now far less personal. The dynamic has completely changed, yet the culture has not changed with them. Meanwhile, employees who were used to an active level of support will feel abandoned and lack direction. Everything will be completely out of balance.

It's hard to argue against the benefits of supporting employees to encourage engagement, but this should never be to the complete exclusion of challenge in the workplace. Without challenge, an organisation is placed at a competitive disadvantage. Let me demonstrate this by using the example of the recent trend aiming to engage employees by significantly improving their work/life balance via initiatives such as a shorter working day or even week. While it's absolutely clear that this has a hugely positive impact on employee engagement, there is perhaps room for discussion as to whether this level of support has gone too far. While there can't be any workforce on the planet that wouldn't delight in ending the week at 5 o'clock on a Thursday afternoon, I'm pretty sure there will always be dozens of competitors motoring on and pushing through hard until the weekend. That seems like an obvious moment to pause, take a breath and consider adopting a more balanced approach to employee engagement.

Like all of the leadership spectrums covered in Part One of this book, it is all about getting the balance right – a balance that keeps the advantages of both challenging and supportive leadership, and distances itself from the disadvantages. Interestingly, I think most people will have experienced the perfect balance in this respect during their school days. Indeed, nearly everyone I have ever spoken to about the challenging–supportive spectrum has immediately piped up to tell me about a teacher who inspired them. Some people even talk about teachers who have changed the entire course of their lives. Why? Well, somehow, these inspirational teachers get the tone just right between being supportive and yet challenging. They shy away from being too supportive because they know full well that the teachers who do this are always taken advantage of. These are the ones who will accept the 'dog ate my homework' excuses with a resigned smile and an utterance of 'Never mind, bring it in tomorrow.' If, on the other hand, a teacher is too strict, the homework will be done and the class apparently attentive, but underneath it all everyone will be too fearful to properly engage. The right balance is somewhere in between. This is where a teacher pushes their pupils when they need to be pushed, but also recognises when they are on edge and can't be pushed any further for the moment. They introduce tough, stretching challenges, but offer just the right level of encouragement when it is required. It's a really difficult balance to achieve, but for those teachers that manage it, the results are transformational. They really can, and do, change lives.

THE THREE ZONES OF DELEGATION

The example of challenge versus support among school-aged children raises some interesting questions. Children, and in particular teenagers, can be tricky customers when it comes to challenge. It is very easy to send them scurrying in the other direction to avoid any hint of (what they take to be) criticism.

By the same token, their inclination is to remain in their comfort zone, where they know they are in no danger of being called out for not achieving. My hunch is that, as we get older, we tend to want to be stretched more – or certainly become more willing to push ourselves and more likely to perform at our best when we are motivated by a mix of challenge and support. When we are asked to do something, we all tend to have our own in-built barometer that decides our personal response to the request. As we can see in Figure 7, the potential reactions can be broken down into three distinct zones. The first is 'comfort', where a team member is completely within their comfort zone and 100% happy to take on the allotted task. In the next stage, stretch, the task may seem unfamiliar and will pull them away from the comfort of their usual day-to-day routine. This means the task may require a certain amount of hand-holding or oversight from the person awarding the task. The final stage, panic, is one that any leader needs to keep a close eye on if this is how their team member responds. Left unchecked, this has

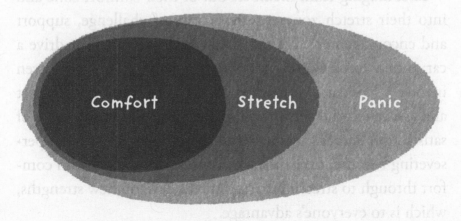

Figure 7. The three zones of pressure for development

the potential to grow into a larger problem, affecting the way the team member feels about their entire job.

Leaders need to be very aware of the responses of individual team members when they delegate tasks. If there is never any challenge involved, people will stagnate and remain in their comfort zone. And, by the same token, if they are over-supported, they will have little incentive to do much more than stay in their comfort zone. This inevitably leads to complacency and sluggish performance. Again, more stagnation. Growth won't occur while everyone is safely tucked up in their comfort zone. Growth of individuals, and an organisation as a whole, only happens when people are stretched. In an ideal world, leaders will regularly challenge their team members to help them out of their comfort zone, in order for them to progress their career by trying something new or more difficult than they are used to. Of course, when a leader pushes people into the stretch zone, they need to take care not to shove them onto the next zone: panic. That's when things start to fall apart.

Encouraging team members out of their comfort zone and into their stretch zone requires a mix of challenge, support and encouragement. It's rather like learning to ski or drive a car; it may feel awkward and unnatural at first, and may even involve a few daring manoeuvres, but with the right support and assistance, the person will master the skill. A huge sense of satisfaction and engagement will then follow. It is worth persevering because, over time, the process of moving from comfort through to stretch helps people to develop new strengths, which is to everyone's advantage.

The majority of employees want to work and, indeed, work

hard. It's within the skill of a good leader to create a balance by enabling a supportive, engaging environment but also pushing the team out of their comfort zone by challenging them and stretching their abilities. This process is helped by clear communication and explicit direction matched by strong, clear feedback. This is the perfect mix of challenge and support.

It is also worth noting here that, in this context, challenge is not a one-way street – or, at least, it shouldn't be. For a team to function properly, team members need to feel able to have unfiltered, passionate debates about things that matter. There needs to be an environment where individuals can openly express opinions and question decisions about their move into the stretch zone, particularly where they believe the result will be unproductive. This is not to advocate a kind of corporate anarchy, where the allocation of every task is met by some sort of free-for-all. However, for the things that truly matter, where the individuals concerned have a valid interest, there needs to be a forum for honest discussion and debate. This doesn't mean to say that a consensus needs to be reached each time. That would be impossible. However, everyone should be heard. Leaders need to be comfortable with their ideas being challenged a little. Once more, if that happened all the time, it would be exhausting and unproductive, but it is something that can and should be encouraged at appropriate moments.

It's important to remember that while, yes, every employee does want to be happy and enjoy their job, many people want to be challenged and stretched too. People enjoy mastering new skills and taking on challenges. It is energising to try

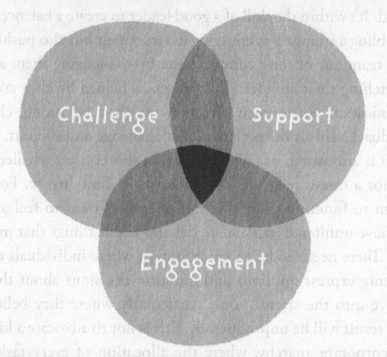

Figure 8. The sweet spot between challenge, support and engagement

things that don't initially come easily. As we can see in Figure 8, there is definitely a sweet spot in the middle of challenge, support and employee engagement.

Although people need to be pushed out of their comfort zone, the exact terms in which bosses couch these efforts will make a difference. Timing, too, is key. Often, the moment when challenging and supportive behaviour collide is when someone on the team feels overloaded or overwhelmed. Recognising the signs initially requires some emotional intelligence, where a leader needs to 'read the room' and see which of their colleagues is not coping well. This is where the approach needs to shift from overtly challenging to one that demonstrates more support.

Reading the room and then shifting approach is not always easy. Most people who are not achieving what they are expected to achieve – or, at least, don't feel their performance is up to par – are very unlikely to want to admit that fact, and certainly not to their boss. They'll be fearful that such an admission will affect their career prospects or see them moved to another, less important role. Thus, a good, supportive leader has to dig in and walk the tightrope between asking questions that may sound challenging but that are needed to draw out what is actually going on, and also showing that they understand the pressures involved and are keen to be of help and assistance to the individual.

The technique that works well here is open questions. Open questions are ones that require more than one-word answers and that can't be quickly shut down with a 'yes' or 'no' answer like their opposite number, closed questions. Open questions are accordion-like: rather than putting people on the spot, they invite responses where the questionee is compelled to be more expansive and reveal more about themselves. A challenging yet supportive open-ended conversation with a colleague who's buckling under pressure might include questions such as:

- 'I've noticed that there is an issue with X project. Can you tell me what might be behind that?'

or

- 'X project seems to be running a little behind schedule. What do you think needs to be done to bring it up to speed?'

These questions are challenging, yes, but they are delivered in a supportive way. They also open up the opportunity for the individual being asked the question to expand on the story behind the situation. The real skill behind asking open-ended questions is to let the person on the receiving end answer. This might sound like the school of the bleeding obvious, but questioners often fail at this. This kind of inquiry is not easy to answer, so it may take time for the responses to come. Most human beings feel awkward when silence stretches between them and the person they are conversing with, and they can't help but leap in to try to fill the void. Don't!

Overall, the goal is to create an environment that makes having tough, challenging talks a little bit easier. If the team is properly supported, they will approach conversations like this with openness, not fear. There is always a fine line when attempting to achieve a balance between challenge and support, but the goal is for everyone to understand that leadership genuinely wants everyone to succeed.

QUESTIONS

To help judge your natural inclination on a scale between centralised control and delegation *see* Table 3. Decide where you sit on each spectrum, where 1 means you strongly agree with the first statement, 2 means you somewhat agree with the first statement, 3 means you agree with each statement about equally, 4 means you somewhat agree with the second statement and 5 means you strongly agree with the second statement. There are no wrong answers – this is simply a guide to help you reflect and perhaps adjust where required.

Challenging	1	2	3	4	5	Supportive
I am comfortable having frank conversations about my team members' performance	1	2	3	4	5	I would prefer not to have performance management conversations with my people
I believe that you have to push people hard to get the best out of them. Motivation is extrinsic.	1	2	3	4	5	I don't believe people have to be pushed hard to get the best out of them. Motivation is intrinsic.
I am comfortable giving and receiving feedback	1	2	3	4	5	I don't like giving or receiving feedback, it's a part of my role that I try to avoid
I believe that challenging goals and high standards get the best out of people	1	2	3	4	5	I believe that providing a supportive environment gets the best out of people
Leaders should remain detached from their teams	1	2	3	4	5	Leaders should be immersed in their teams

Table 3. Challenging and Supportive

CHAPTER FIVE
PROCESSES — CREATIVITY

There is a widely accepted narrative about leadership that praises creativity and innovation. Commentators speak breathlessly about visionaries who have big ideas and push them through, changing everything around them and their organisation forever. These are (it is said) the people with the imagination to sweep aside rigid structures, solve problems by seeing things in a way that others don't and take entirely new perspectives. Indeed, one survey listed 'creativity' as the *most important* leadership quality, with 60% of respondents rating it this way, over and above integrity, global thinking and openness. Fairness lagged a long way behind in the league table of leadership qualities, at 12%![10]

Creativity is, of course, only half the picture. Somehow, someone – or several someones – has to implement all those great ideas and make them a reality. To do this, a structured, measured approach is required. In other words, standards and processes need to be deployed.

10 'IBM 2010 Global CEO Study: Creativity selected as most crucial factor for future success' (IBM, 18 May 2020), https://www.-03.ibm.com/press/us/en/pressrelease/31670.wss.

STANDARD OPERATING PROCEDURES

Though often unfairly maligned as boring or bureaucratic, processes are an essential part of the business mix. The beauty of processes is that they tell everyone what is going to happen, when and how. They provide clarity about what 'good' looks like. They describe the specific steps that need to be taken to get from point A to point B, safely and efficiently. They are the clear set of instructions on the optimum way to do a task.

As you might expect, the military is hugely reliant on standard operating procedures (SOPs), which, if you were to boil them down to one overarching principle, mean that there is a single best way to do something at a given point in time (standards can always be improved). Recruits of all ranks are taught to use written SOP instructions and then drilled, so that following these clearly-laid-out processes becomes second nature. The core of the principle is broadly similar when it is applied in the workplace too, and there are some very good reasons why. At the bare minimum, process ensures consistency, reduced errors, improved communication and compliance.

The more consistent a process is, regardless of the person being tasked to do it, the fewer chances there are of quality issues. When you visit McDonald's or Burger King, you can fully expect that your favourite burger will taste exactly like your favourite burger, whether you order one in Southend, Seattle or Sydney. And quite rightly. You've grown to like and appreciate your preferred choice and you'd be pretty disappointed if the recipe changed, even subtly, or the wrong topping was applied. It's thanks to standards and processes that you can count on getting the same product time and time again, regardless of who is flipping that burger. It's why we trust these established organisations. Granted, when products fail to meet expectations, a customer's level of frustration with an organisation will very much depend on the amount they have invested in the said product. For example, the measure of dissatisfaction around a £20 steak being poorer than billed will be far deeper and longer lasting than that encountered when a £2 burger is found to be below par. Nevertheless, no company can afford to regularly underperform in this respect. Indeed, arguably, no business should ever allow any inconsistencies whatsoever to creep into its output. This is a sure-fire route to losing loyal customers.

When there are written standards and processes, where the various stages of a task are precisely documented, it doesn't just reduce the potential for error; it also makes things more straightforward for the team. A good example of this would be the way a surgeon practises their trade. This medical professional will have been trained over many, many hours, rehearsing and re-rehearsing proven techniques that will then be perfectly replicated in the operating theatre. In certain cases, there is a little leeway allowed, such as if the surgeon finds something when they open up a patient and the initial diagnosis changes. However, this means they will then switch from one process to another, in order to deal with the new issue. There is certainly no possibility of a surgeon going 'freestyle' as they seek to deal with a change in a patient's outlook. Their only use of creativity is to switch between processes as and when required.

Central to the efficient execution of standards and processes is accurate communication, because this is how an organisation conveys a complete roadmap of how to do things, even if a task is quite complex. Say, for example, a company is planning a significant software purchase. In this case, it would make a lot of sense to have a process in place to properly evaluate the strengths and weaknesses of the proposed software package. This should, among other things, involve a full checklist of the features required, which is essential information that will be needed to make the best evaluation. If there is nothing to compare the software to, or no clear brief, the possibilities for error are endless.

As usual, the communication should go both ways. If there are gaps in the process or an element doesn't work as billed, there should be a mechanism to enable team members to flag this, so the process can be tightened up. I once worked with a team where this didn't happen as it should and the outcome was chaotic. The operations manager, who had devised the process, and who was arguably too close to it all, took it to heart when he overheard colleagues discussing an issue with the process. He completely flew off the handle and the resulting fall-out from his reaction took nearly 48 hours to resolve. When the manager finally calmed down (and apologised to his rather upset colleagues), he did admit that there were issues and made the required changes. Being open to hearing feedback from users is an essential element of effective processes.

There are numerous areas in any type of business that benefit from the organised thinking brought about by following processes. Any company that is heavily reliant on making things, for example, will need to effectively communicate processes for every stage of the production line. As well as being essential for maintaining quality control and ensuring customers always receive goods to a consistent quality and specifications, as per the burger example previously mentioned, processes make sure production lines work smoothly. After all, shut-downs and outages resulting from equipment failure or a shortage of supplies are costly.

If things change and processes are updated, new standards can be documented and provided to the team. If the changes are sufficiently complex, everyone can be given clear, informative training so they have a complete understanding about what needs to be done.

Written processes also provide a handy checklist for employees old and new. During annual reviews, processes are a useful measure of job performance too. They are also an important part of making sure any business looks after its workforce and environment, and they are crucial for compliance. All organisations are subject to laws and regulations, whatever sector they operate in, with some subject to more stringent rules than others. Processes ensure these obligations are satisfied, and they are also confirmation of a company's good-faith intention to operate within these rules. This is, of course, about so much more than simply complying with statutory obligations regarding health and safety, the environment or financial regulations. Documented processes are essential when it comes to avoiding accidents, fines and potential litigation, which can be hugely damaging to any business. All of that is before you get to the potential PR disasters of spills, emissions or any of a number of calamities that may threaten the community in the immediate vicinity, or loyal long-term customers. If the worst does happen, processes will also come into their own if there is an investigation. They are a historical, factual record of the steps in an existing process.

Figure 9 is a good representation of the importance of

STANDARDS AND CONTINUOUS IMPROVEMENT

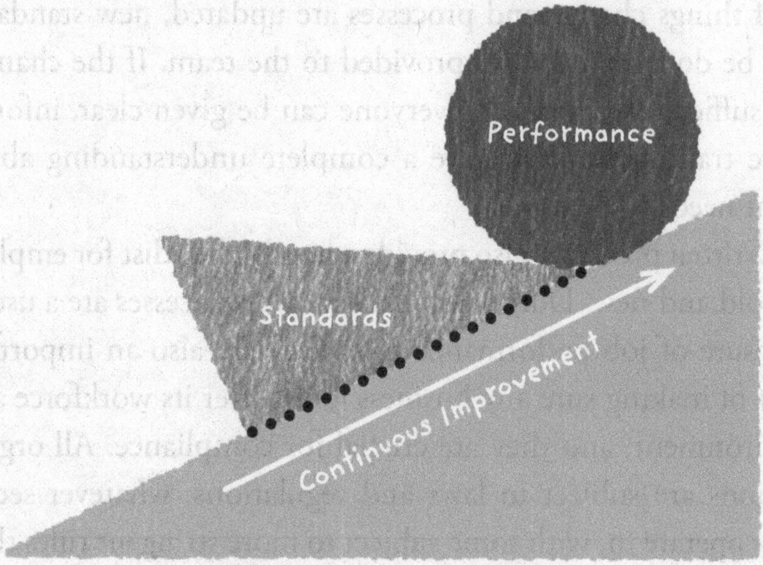

Figure 9. Standards and processes

standards and processes in all respects of a business's performance. They are like a wedge that locks in performance. If you don't have these standards firmly in place, performance will soon start to slip or roll downhill. The dotted line on the graphic depicts the act of leaders checking standards; if they miss out this vital step, standards will begin to slip. In every high-performing organisation that Roderic and I have ever worked in, the leader has regularly 'walked the floor' to make sure the highest version of the standards is being adhered to.

Process confirmation, or the act of confirming that the processes you've created are being adhered to, is a core leadership behaviour. Take away the wedge, and things will go wrong very quickly. Once that downward momentum begins, it will be very hard to stop.

FLEX YOUR CREATIVE MUSCLE EVERY DAY

While we have, I believe, shown that standards and processes cannot be ignored, what about the exciting process of coming up with ideas? We are talking about those creative steps forward that can transform an organisation from something not particularly special to one that leaves its competitors in its wake. That's what leadership is paid the big bucks for, right? The ability to create something novel and interesting to please and delight customers is, after all, the lifeblood of a growing business.

There is absolutely no doubt at all that we all need to be in the practice of regularly thinking about new and better ways of doing things. As American entrepreneur and angel investor James Altucher has said, creativity is like a muscle that needs to be flexed every day.[11] He practises what he preaches too, seeking to write down ten new ideas on a daily basis. These ideas can be anything from a new business model to a different way of doing something mundane. His view is that by the seventh

11   James Altucher, 'The ultimate guide for becoming an idea machine' (James Altucher, 14 May 2014), https:// jamesaltucher.com/blog/the-ultimate-guide-for-becoming-an-idea-machine.

idea of the day, it can become really, really difficult. However, he pushes through because it forces him to keep flexing that creativity muscle. It is effective too, because people have grown some multi-million-dollar companies on the back of Altucher's daily musings.

It does also need to be said that there are a lot of misunderstandings about creativity.

Frequently, when people talk admiringly about creativity, they focus on the myth of the lone inventor. This is the creative genius who comes up with an awe-inspiring breakthrough that changes the world forever. In reality, this is actually quite rare. For a start, there are very few breakthroughs of this scale. Most are incremental improvements (of which more later). Also, truly creative companies are innovative thanks to a culture of creativity (i.e. *lots* of inventors coming up with ideas). This is where a range of people across different disciplines collaborate on an idea to tackle a problem and make things work better.

Perhaps the most important starting point when you consider innovation is that it doesn't have to be all about producing an entirely new, ground-breaking idea, every time. Indeed, endeavouring to maintain the momentum via a scattergun approach may mean you never come up with one meaningful idea to develop at all. James Dyson is a really interesting example of how it is possible to be incredibly creative, but also intensely focused on process and the end goal. The story of the inventor's quest to make the perfect vacuum cleaner, which lead to 15 years of strife and 5127 prototypes, is well known. What is not commented on so much is what happened next – certainly not in the context of creativity. Now, here was a person who was clearly not afraid to think the big thoughts and dream the big dreams. Yet, rather than haring off in another direction entirely to find his next invention, his mindset stayed very close to home. I'm not privy to his actual thought process, but it seems to me it might have gone something like this: *what am I good at?* How has the Dyson company made its name? The answer is, on a very basic level, that the business became a billion-dollar company on the back of its ability to move air around better than any other company on the planet. The 'cyclone' technology perfected for the innovative Dyson vacuum cleaners was the reason for its success. All that business needed to do was to apply that technology to another product group that needed updating. Again, I'm not presuming to follow the thought processes of the British inventor, but perhaps his mind turned to the number of men seen exiting loos and wiping their recently washed hands on their jeans. Hand driers just never seem to work in these public facilities! Here was a problem that could be solved with the judicious use of high-pressure air. And so, the Dyson Airblade hand drier was invented. Another product that may have been subject to a similar thought process was the humble hairdryer. Again, the design had not changed or been improved upon in years. The Dyson organisation brought its knowledge of air movement to hair drying and reinvented another product group with the release of the Dyson Supersonic.

What the Dyson example shows about creativity is that it is a combination of thinking truly innovative thoughts and then enacting incremental improvements to achieve a goal. James Dyson didn't start with goal of 'improving' the vacuum cleaner, or hand or hair driers; he wanted to completely reinvent them and was entirely prepared to throw out the original models that someone else had created and start again. This is often known as 'first principles thinking'. This is different from where many organisations begin, focusing on improving what they have. Once you have shifted into the new territory of first principles thinking, you can begin to make the incremental moves to turn your idea into the best possible version of itself.

Incremental improvement wins the day when it comes to standards and processes. An effective illustration of how the way things are done can and should be steadily improved is the world record for the men's high jump. More than 100 years ago, in 1912, George Horine set the record, with a jump of 2 metres, using a technique he'd devised called the 'western roll'. At the time there was a strict 'no diving' rule in place, so Horine spent many months of experimentation trying to come up with a viable alternative. The one he settled upon was to change the direction of approach so the take-off leg was nearer to the bar. The next big leap (if you'll excuse the pun) in high jump development came around 1935, when some jumpers adopted a straddle jump, which saw the record edge up to 2.07 metres and then steadily rise centimetre by centimetre from there.

The real game changer, though, came in July 1968, when Dick Fosbury won the high jump gold medal at the Mexico City Olympics. Not long before this event, there had been one of those periodic improvements to the equipment for the sport, which had been little remarked upon. These are the sorts of things that happen all the time. Earlier, for example, there had been changes to the pegs the high jump bar sat on, to stop jumpers exploiting a loophole where they could hit the bar hard without dislodging it. In this particular case, it was a modification to the landing area that captured Fosbury's attention. Previously, high jumpers had alighted on a fairly sparse mat. Now, though, what awaited them on the other side of the high jump bar was a large, far more padded mattress-style landing area, which was much, much softer. Many people may not have thought much about the difference at the time; however, when an environment changes, it gives you space to try something different. And that is exactly what Fosbury did, with his now famous 'Fosbury flop'. When he first showcased the technique, everyone was mystified. Some people even laughed. But then he won the gold medal and everyone had to sit up and take notice. Indeed, everyone in the sport has adopted the technique ever since. Today's high jumpers are leaping in excess of 2.45 metres. I wonder what George Horine would have said if anyone had told him that, a century on from his record-breaking leap, people would apparently be defying gravity to leap almost 25% higher.

This high jump progression is a really great example of the symbiotic relationship between process and innovation. Fosbury had completely the right mindset when it came to approaching how to improve the process. He was constantly asking: is this the best way to do this now? How has the environment changed? Can I make improvements?

CREATIVITY VERSUS CONSOLIDATION

Creativity for creativity's sake is not always a good thing. If the leadership becomes too relentless in their innovating, it'll be exhausting for everyone around them. It could well become counterproductive too, because everyone will begin to have change fatigue. Pushing the boundaries is great, but new ideas need time to be examined and implemented. They need to be given space to bed down if they are to have a chance to be effective. Any leader who consistently tries to change things will quickly use up all their leadership capital, however exciting and innovative their thought processes are. There are only so many interventions that can be made before they all appear to run into one, completely losing their power and potency. Teams learn from constant about-faces, where leaders pivot from one idea to the next. After a while, they just don't bother to put in much effort when a 'ground-breaking concept' is presented. What's the point? Like buses, there will be another one along in a minute. At the very least, there will start to be some serious pushback.

I came across a great example of this while working with a hugely acquisitive chief executive. This person was consumed by the idea of accelerating the growth of her business though numerous mergers. She put together and enacted a number of quite innovative pairings in a very short space of time. Now, as everyone who operates at the sharp end of business knows, the process of buying a company is very intense and the integration that follows can be long and painful, requiring a lot of work. This is certainly so if the purchase is of any significant size and the incumbent company already has well-established processes and systems of its own. Where the acquisition process can really break down is when the board negotiates and approves a purchase, but then immediately hands it over to the operations team with the missive to 'make it work' while they get on with eyeing up the next exciting acquisition prospect. This can cause a huge problem. The operations team will be running themselves ragged and will need time to do their stuff, as well as needing support from the top. So, if the leadership team turns around and says that there will be more integration to follow shortly thanks to the next looming acquisition, just as this chief executive did time and again, things will begin to fall apart very quickly.

For many businesses, the plea to put on the brakes and consolidate what is already happening flies in the face of the school of thought that companies need to be in constant motion, relentlessly casting out new ideas. While acquisition is a process, it is one that is often at odds with the day-to-day processes of an organisation, and it was difficult to get this chief executive to see my alternative point of view that the constant need to bed in new companies was disruptive. Eventually, though, I was able to persuade her that ongoing momentum might sound impressive, but the rhetoric does not always match the reality. There needs to be a period of calm and the space to create processes to accommodate all these great ideas.

Innovation is, of course, only innovative when creative ideas are actually implemented. The real danger of a deluge of ideas is that *nothing at all* will actually get properly executed. Another chief executive I knew created a classic environment for this scenario. He was well known for basing his assessment of his team on the quantity of ideas they brought forth. Each year, like clockwork, he'd gather his top team around him and invite them to brainstorm ideas for ways to close the annual funding gap that consistently left the organisation down by a few million pounds. Initially, the team would enthusiastically pitch in with numerous money-spinning concepts, many of which were hugely innovative, and all of which the chief executive would lap up and praise at the session. But that was as far as it would go. No one was ever charged with actually executing the innovative ideas and, not surprisingly, nothing changed. In fact, no one even spoke of what had been said until the exercise was repeated the following year. Hardly surprisingly, the brainstorming sessions became less and less creative. The hearts of the team simply weren't in the sessions. They were a waste of time. While (initially at least) they produced a hugely creative pot of ideas, progress ground to a halt because there was no process to follow them up. No one was assigned to tasks, so no one could be held accountable for not making things happen.

Ideas alone are nothing. If you don't have the skills to execute them or aren't capable of enabling your team to do so, there is no value in the ideas whatsoever. The obvious answer is to create a balance between thinkers who come up with the ideas, and doers who get the proverbial done. This is why creativity and process are such brilliant bedfellows. It's fantastic for someone to come in brimming with out-of-the-box ideas every day, but the people around them have to be able to say 'yes, that will work' or 'no, that won't' – and why. Most importantly, if they do judge that something could work, they will have the focus and understanding to deliver, and then find the processes so the whole team can get behind the idea and go on delivering. The more complex the idea, the more skills will be required to execute it, which means more people will inevitably be required to be involved in the process. If it is not well thought through, chaos will reign supreme.

One of my most extreme illustrations of how well this combination can work in practice occurred during my first job after leaving the army, when I began working for a chain of private-member business clubs. The clubs themselves were very plush and discrete – completely set up for those small, very private conversations that need to go on each day to keep the world of commerce moving smoothly. One of the partners who ran the clubs was the archetypical Duracell Bunny when it came to creativity. He would burst in each day, brimming with ideas for ways to make the club better for its guests. It was fairly apparent that he had barely slept the night before because he was always visibly shaking from the pressure of the geyser of ideas that were welling up inside him, waiting to pour forth. And what ideas they were. It was exhausting just listening to them when he presented a rapid download of them upon his arrival in the club's offices. His business partner was the complete opposite in every way. He would stand there, completely impassively, listening to the ideas, only occasionally interjecting to say quietly that this or that would not work. Eventually, the tensions between the two would invariably reach fever pitch and a heated conversation would ensue. The fall-out from the emotional explosion would be that the pair would agree that perhaps one of the many ideas might be explored more fully, and the quieter partner would disappear and focus on putting the processes in place to bring it to life. It was a terrifying daily event, run in the midst of a dizzying amount of stress and tension, but it seemed to work.

Neither of these characters was wrong in their approach (not that they would have changed even if they had been told that they were). The balance of their particular skills, creativity and focus on processes was crucial in keeping the business growing and moving forward.

WHAT DOES 'GOOD' LOOK LIKE?

There is always room for creativity in business. Trying different ways of doing things is to be encouraged. After all, how do you gain a competitive edge if you are doing the same as everyone else? Any organisation that comes up with a way of doing things and then carries on doing the same thing, day in and day out, will very quickly find itself losing ground and becoming irrelevant.

It is important to set standards, but it is equally important to continually challenge them. As the context changes, the processes must change as required. This will require some degree of creative thinking in order to answer that important question: is there a better way of doing this?

Creativity is always led from the top. It would be counterproductive to have a free-for-all, where everyone on the team could try out their own ideas on a whim. Creativity needs to be carefully controlled to avoid customers encountering an unfamiliar and untested product, which they may not take kindly to. Can you imagine what would happen if the barista in Starbucks suddenly decided to go freestyle with your mocha? However, while creativity is controlled from the top, it is crucial to take the team with you. Leaders should regularly ask their team for input on what 'good' should look like. What so often happens in organisations is that these things are not talked about. Friction is created and people fall out, but at no point have people had a sensible conversation along these lines: 'what is your expectation about X process? Meanwhile, let me explain what my expectations are.' As soon as people do that, a real lightbulb moment ensues.

Get your team used to the concept by regularly prompting an examination of what good looks like. When a meeting ends, pose the question: was that a good meeting? This inevitably leads on to the question of, well, what does 'good' look like in a meeting context? Doing this forces people to sit down and think about what they actually want from a meeting. No one wants to sit through countless meetings that are a complete waste of time. Find out whether the meeting attendees have fallen into the trap of simply sharing information. What would be their recommendations on improvements that would actually change the way you do business? Soon, interrogating what 'good' actually looks like will start to become a habit. All processes will begin to be scrutinised in this way. Take sales as an example. A salesperson can be challenged to analyse why they won a particular sale within this context. By deconstructing the process, they will discover the secret sauce that got the client signing on the dotted line. If they can do this, it will be hugely helpful when it comes to training others on the team with whatever innovation worked so well. It becomes part of the process. And, as a consequence, everyone can better perform what 'good' looks like in sales. Very soon, the team will get to a position where the new behaviour is locked in.

The success of this endeavour relies on the engagement of the team, which means they need to be sure that their suggestions will be given a good hearing. It's not an easy balance to pull off. On the one hand, they'll have been told that they need to rigidly stick to certain processes, but then on the other they are being asked whether they can see a better way. It's worth making the effort to invite input, though, because the people who use the processes are in the best place to put forward ideas on how to do the same processes faster, more efficiently or with fewer steps. Certainly, you don't want to be running an organisation where people regularly gather around the water cooler to complain about the inefficiencies of certain processes but are never given a forum to share their solutions.

Flexibility between process and creativity and the goal of continuous improvement is hugely important. If you adopt a standard and stick with it no matter what, you are pretty much a bureaucrat. (Certainly, if you ever find yourself saying, or even thinking, 'this is the way we've always done things', that is the time to pause.) Doing nothing is a really dangerous strategy. Processes need to be balanced with a policy of constantly looking for more innovative ways of doing things.

QUESTIONS

To help judge your natural inclination on a scale between centralised control and delegation *see* Table 4 on the following page. Decide where you sit on each spectrum, where 1 means you strongly agree with the first statement, 2 means you somewhat agree with the first statement, 3 means you agree with each statement about equally, 4 means you somewhat agree with the second statement and 5 means you strongly agree with the second statement. There are no wrong answers – this is simply a guide to help you reflect and perhaps adjust where required.

	1	2	3	4	5	
I believe that good processes are essential to the effective running of an organisation	1	2	3	4	5	I believe that processes tend to stifle creativity
There is always a 'best way' to do something	1	2	3	4	5	There is not always a 'best way' to do something
Most solutions come from the creation of a clear and easy to follow process	1	2	3	4	5	Most solutions come from a creative approach to solving a problem
Leaders are responsible for confirming processes are adhered to	1	2	3	4	5	Leaders should not waste time on checking processes are being followed
I find it easier to execute a plan rather than come up with ideas	1	2	3	4	5	I find it easier to come up with ideas rather than execute a plan

Table 4. Processes and Creativity

CHAPTER SIX
BIG PICTURE — IN THE DETAIL

The story of the journey to gold medal victory at the Sydney Olympics made by the British men's Rowing Eight sums up the process and effectiveness of big-picture thinking. Ben Hunt-Davis described the power of this concept to a tee in the title of the book he co-wrote about it: *Will it Make the Boat Go Faster?*[12] Every single action and process in the months and years running up to the global competition was measured against that one question (see Figure 10). Those seven words summed up what mattered most to the rowing team and, once they had articulated it, everything they did as individuals and as a team was measured against the goal and adjusted and improved accordingly. Often those improvements would just be on a small, incremental basis, but if anything whatsoever was considered not to be moving the boat on, it was immediately dispensed with. The singular goal forced the team to interrogate each action to see whether it was effective. If they were doing endurance training, what did each exercise add? If they were practising sprints, how much did that process improve their speed? Simply training hard was not good enough. They

---

12 Harriet Beveridge and Ben Hunt-Davis, *Will it Make the Boat Go Faster?* Olympic-Winning Strategies for Everyday Success (Leicester: Matador, 2011).

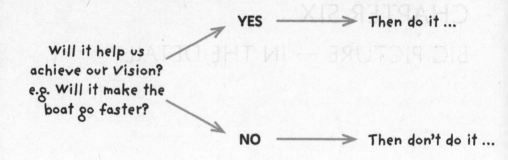

Figure 10. Measuring the effectiveness of actions

needed to evaluate each action to make sure it was making a difference. The beauty of this attitude to training was that the big goal forced the whole team to focus relentlessly.

The same logic can, and indeed should, be applied to any organisation. A big picture means you have created a compelling vision for the whole team. It might be a bold statement or a graphic depicting where the organisation expects to be in two, three or five years' time. The end game is the same: it is a target that forces everyone in the team to begin thinking about how to achieve what needs to be done. Everything that happens next is viewed through that big-picture filter, pushing the organisation ever further towards that goal.

My own experience of the effectiveness of this big-picture focus happened while I worked at Henderson Global Investors as Global Head of Leadership and Learning. The international fund management group had launched a new strategy under the title of 'Growth and Globalisation'. The reason for that strategy? They needed to grow the firm and they wanted to do so by expanding globally. It was as simple as that. What they did so well was to succinctly put this clarion call for action down on a single slide, which was shown again and again to everyone on the team. Accompanying the Growth and Globalisation goal was a brief summary distilling the message down into a brief bit of text that gave a clear direction of travel. It simply stated why the organisation existed, what it wanted to achieve and what the metrics were. From the day this strategy was revealed to everyone in the organisation, the firm worked really hard on focusing attention on the key messages and making sure everyone was exposed to them as often as possible. The slide was shown at every single internal and external presentation. It was used and it was lived, extensively. Every leader was encouraged to constantly ask the question: is what you are doing, and what your team is doing, contributing to this goal? If it isn't, stop it, or change it so it does contribute. It was powerful stuff. I frequently heard my colleagues using this metric to question the value of activities, and everyone instantly understood why they were being asked the question.

Pursuing a collective goal is not a negative strategy. You are not stopping people from doing things. No one felt in the least bit frustrated when they were pulled up on something that had veered away from the Growth and Globalisation goal. They knew that was what they were there to achieve and understood the focus.

Organisations that focus on a single strategy in this way are better off when it comes to attracting, motivating and retaining employees. To continue the story about Henderson's Growth and Globalisation for a moment, there was another example of just how powerful the one-goal message was. I spoke with many people who joined the firm long after the vision was first announced and widely disseminated, and they told me that they had joined *because of it*. They were impressed that the firm was so clear about what it wanted to achieve and wanted to be part of it.

It is the same reason why so many people are inspired to work for Elon Musk. The entrepreneur has set out a big, hairy, audacious goal to 'send 1 million people to Mars by 2050'[13] by launching three Starship rockets every day to the red planet. Not surprisingly, he has many, many of the world's finest minds knocking on his door and wanting to be part of this exciting project. Teams want clarity and focus. They relish working towards an interesting and measurable goal, with a clear timeline for achieving it.

Something that we find very interesting is that Musk has been entirely focused on his own goals since his days at university. In the nineties, while at the University of Pennsylvania, where he spent three years doing a degree in science, and a further year studying economics, he set out to answer the question of what things would most affect the future of humanity so he could focus his career around them.

The five elements he homed in on were the internet, sustainable energy, space exploration, artificial intelligence and rewriting human genetics. Anyone who has followed his career will realise that every move has been connected with this aim,

13 Morgan McFall-Johnsen and Dave Mosher, 'Elon Musk says he plans to send 1 million people to Mars by 2050 by launching 3 Starship rockets every day and creating "a lot of jobs" on the red planet' (*Business Insider*, 17 January 2020), https://www.businessinsider.com/elon-musk-plans-1-million-people-to-mars-by-2050-2020-1?r=US&IR=T.

from the online payment company PayPal to the electric car maker Tesla to the solar energy business SolarCity to SpaceX.

Once an organisation (or individual) has a big-picture goal, it can get into the detail and plan what needs to be done and the various steps that must be taken on a day-to-day basis to achieve it. What are the behaviours that are required to get there? The value of big-picture thinking is that it creates a boundary for everyone to innovate within. Everyone can be told: *use your creativity – come to me with ideas on how to make this happen.*

Having clarity and something to aim for is crucial to keep teams on track on a day-to-day basis, but it can really help when something unexpected happens too. One time, a company I was working for had been invited into a major bank to pitch for some work. Our invitation to the meeting had come on the back of a massive screw-up by another supplier. They'd pitched for a piece of global work and completely failed to deliver the goods. I remember listening to the brief with a growing sense of alarm. The company was fairly small at the time and was very much UK-based, but we had big-picture ambitions for growth. The bank executives were asking us to deliver goods to Lithuania, South Africa and Singapore. Then, almost out of nowhere, I heard the commercial director speak from the chair next to me.

'Yes, absolutely, we can do that,' he said, calmly. 'We've got a broad network of associates that we work with.'

It was all I could do to stop myself swinging around in my chair to challenge him on this confident assertion. *What associates?!*

My feeling of rising panic was interrupted by the effusive approval of one of the bank executives.

'Great, well in that case, the job is yours,' he said, before going on to wrap up the meeting by discussing a few of the logistical matters we'd need to know.

I waited until we'd got well clear of the bank's headquarters before I challenged my colleague.

'If I hadn't said it, they'd have said no.' He shrugged. 'We'll think of something.'

The big goal was, of course, to set up an international network that would rapidly move us towards our global ambitions, as well as making good on our new contract. It was risky, but it was an informed risk, because we knew it wouldn't be too difficult to find the right teams. What we needed to do next was to get into the detail and work out how to fulfil our promise. In the next few weeks, we had to pedal like fury to set up teams in Lithuania, South Africa and Singapore, but we managed it. It turned out to be a great piece of business too and led to a great deal of expansion elsewhere. By focusing on the big picture, we were able to ignore distractions and get the job done.

EVERYONE NEEDS TO BE ON BOARD

Big-picture targets are crucial for any business. Individuals want to know the big picture, and lack of clarity is often the source of significant disquiet in organisations. Without the big picture (whether there simply isn't one or management has been terrible at conveying the strategy), confusion reigns. If no one knows where they are going, it stands to reason that it is impossible to head off in the right direction. Individuals on the team might try to compensate for the lack of input by putting forward their own ideas, but it is inevitable that the reception these ideas receive will be very much dependent on what is going through the leader's head at that particular moment. After all, if the person at the top has no big picture, they have no metric against which to measure the team.

It is worth noting that the term 'big picture' has different connotations depending on where you are in an organisation. Imagine, for example, the admin side of a manufacturing business. At a lower level, there is the accounts department, and the bigger picture to the half a dozen or so people there means keeping an accurate track of accounts receivable and accounts payable. Their line manager will look across the entire finance department, so that person's banner focus will be broader but still not massive. Higher up in the organisation will be the CFO, who will oversee all areas of company operation, and their bigger picture will be anything that makes a profit or loss. Then, of course, there is the chief executive, who will have to have a good understanding of the financials and also all of the other elements that contribute to the bottom line. The balancing act here is for leaders to fully understand the big-picture challenges at each level, without getting down into the weeds with each team. The person in charge needs to be able to pull away and weigh up all the options. The skill is being able to dip in, but not to get so stuck into it that you can't get out. Figure 11 is a useful example of an organisational vision that Roderic and I worked on with the Bulgari hotel group.

ORGANISATIONAL TO TEAM VISIONS

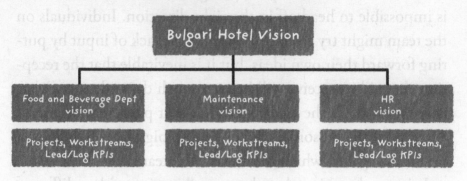

Figure 11. Organisational vision

Focusing on the big picture is not without its challenges. There are plenty of organisations that have been caught out by concentrating *all* of their resources on what they thought was the right goal, when in reality there were other, far more pressing issues to be prioritising. Perhaps the most oft-quoted example of this is Kodak, which was once dominant in photographic film. Thirty years ago, the 'Kodak moment' was a buzzword around the globe. Yet, the organisation was so focused on protecting the value of its intellectual property and patents that it did not spend enough time understanding and embracing the growth in digital photography. This inward-facing, rather than outward-facing, approach undoubtedly contributed a great deal towards the firm sinking into Chapter 11 bankruptcy in 2012. It has since re-emerged under the same name but is a shadow of its former self.

To be fair to Kodak, and others in its position, thinking the big thoughts can also be tricky for large public companies. They are judged on quarterly results and the financial markets can be pretty unforgiving if there are not tangible signs of substantial progress: not an easy thing to pull off for a variety of reasons. This is very vividly illustrated by the experiences of Anthony Jenkins, who was parachuted into Barclays in 2012 to help clean up the bank's act in the wake of scandals such as Libor and foreign exchange rigging. He had a lot to contend with; the bank was still in recovery mode following the 2008/9 financial crisis, jobs needed to be cut, branches were closing, and faith in banks and bankers was low. When he joined, Jenkins was open about the scale of changes in culture that were required to meet his vision for the bank, telling the City the changes would take up to seven years to effect. The City barely gave him three. In among the kind words that surrounded his departure was a very telling comment from the new chairman John McFarlane, who thanked Jenkins for all his excellent work on culture and values: 'As a group, if we aspire to bring shareholder returns forward, we need to be much more focused on what is attractive, what we are good at, and where we are good at it,' McFarlane said.[14]

The City had clearly spoken. Focusing on the bigger picture is very difficult when the markets are demanding solid results on a quarterly basis, or certainly worthwhile incremental improvements. (In certain industry sectors in Australia, this timescale is monthly!) There is little room for manoeuvre, or patience, when setting off on a project that might take two, three or four years to show decent returns, even if those returns are expected to be significant. The market quizzes companies

---

14 Jill Treanor, 'Barclays fires chief executive Antony Jenkins' (*The Guardian*, 8 July 2015), https://www.theguardian.com/business/2015/jul/08/barclays-fires-chief-executive-antony-jenkins.

on what they have achieved in the past few months, rather than giving much consideration to the long game.

IT'S THE DETAIL THAT WILL SHOW YOU HOW TO GET WHERE YOU WANT TO BE

While thinking the big thoughts is vital for leadership, so too is having an understanding of how everyone needs to proceed to get there. This will inevitably require a large number of small steps and, while a leader should never micromanage, they need an overview and understanding of that detail. In any given situation, though, there will be a judgement call about how far into the detail they need to go. These calls are based on a combination of ingrained knowledge, prior experience and a few assumptions.

Some day-to-day decisions require very little thought. They are pretty much along the same lines as if, say, you jumped into an Uber for a trip to the airport. You could make the fair assumption that the driver will get you from A to B. That's their job. There is no need to get into the detail or to make sure they've topped up the oil and windscreen fluids before picking you up. Other actions require closer attention, though. Think along the lines of going under the knife for a big operation. In this instance, you might look a little more closely at your surgeon beforehand. It's likely that you'd want to know their track record and success rate with similar operations.

Gathering the relevant information and asking the right questions are clearly key when it comes to scrutinising the detail. It is very easy to assume you know what is going on and that everyone on the team is focused on the big picture. However, it is crucial, now and again, to check this is exactly what is happening. It's rather like shining a laser light into the heart of a business to check whether it needs any attention and exactly where.

A chief executive I once worked with joined what, on paper at least, looked like a thriving organisation. The sales figures were good, it was at the top of its field and there were no obvious warning signs. However, his first act was to really drill down into the detail of those apparently soaring sales. Who, he asked, were the top performers? Where was the organisation getting the most value from its team? When he looked into the detail, the picture became very different indeed.

There were some people on the team who were light years in front of others in terms of performance. Meanwhile, there were some areas of the business that had been entirely neglected for a very long time. As a result, they were languishing in very negative territory indeed. The number of opportunities being missed was astonishing. This new chief executive used a fresh perspective to ask the right questions to focus on the parts of the organisation that were sorely in need of attention. Arguably, though, the organisation should never have required a fresh set of eyes on the problem. This level of attention to detail should be happening all the time in any business.

Being open to looking at the detail can often allow you to zoom in to make short-term, opportunist moves before zooming back out once more. Leaders who retain an interest in looking around at the here and now, as well as scrutinising the big picture on the horizon, will see a range of immediate opportunities.

Right at the beginning of the coronavirus crisis in 2020, Roderic and I sat down and brainstormed what we could do to ensure that our businesses were in peak condition when we finally came out the other side. Much of our day-to-day work was stalled because of social distancing, so we couldn't run our usual workshops. We therefore agreed that this enforced stay-at-home period was the right time to produce a series of webinars outlining our balanced leadership philosophy. That way, when some sort of normal resumed, we'd be 100% ready to resume business and would have a better offering for our clients too.

While keeping a watchful eye on short-term details is good, it should never become a distraction from keeping an eye on the big-picture goal. Roderic told me an interesting story in this respect, concerning a relative of his who used to work for Jaguar some years ago. Whenever the family went off on their annual summer holiday, camping in France, this fellow would take along every spare part imaginable, pre-empting pretty much anything that might go wrong with the car on the journey. Fortunately, he fully understood the mechanics of his Jag, so diving into the detail seemed justified. (I will make no comment here about the reliability or otherwise of old Jags!) The point here, though, is that there would be little point doing something similar today. Modern cars are entirely different. They are so complex that diving into the detail would be a frustrating waste of time.

DETAIL IS NOT A COMFORT BLANKET!

Leaders need to understand where their time is best used and when it is better to leave the detail to the experts. That doesn't always happen, though. A lot of people at the top of organisations still regularly try to fiddle under the hood, when really they shouldn't be concerning themselves with that aspect of the running of their organisation. I am quite familiar with this scenario from my time in Kenya with the Scots Guards. I worked with a brilliant captain, whom I will call Captain Peters here. The lads all used the nickname *Corporal* Peters, though. Why? Well, whenever we did an exercise, such as live-firing platoon attacks, he would always be right up with the lead section. To clarify, in this sort of exercise, there are three teams. One will be assaulting the position, another will be positioned at 90 degrees to them, firing away to make sure everyone on the other side keeps their heads down, and a third is placed behind them in reserve. Captain Peters was supposed to be somewhere in the middle of all that with an eye on the bigger picture, but he couldn't help inserting himself right into the action with the lead section out in front. He was forever in the wrong place because of his enthusiasm to get things right, trying to insert himself into the detail – hence the nickname. Eventually, the corporal who was actually in charge of the lead section had to tell him to go away and let him do his job. Except he wasn't quite as polite as that!

One situation where you often see leaders embracing the detail a little too much is in areas of a business that they are most familiar with, perhaps one where they formerly had a role. This might happen when they have recently been promoted away from that area to take up a more senior role. The promotion was most likely because the individual proved to be brilliant at being in the detail, with a real understanding of everything that was going on. Unfortunately, what happens is that they are drawn to remaining in that comfort zone thereafter. What they should be doing is focusing on the big picture and encouraging the people below them to work out the incremental steps required to get their department towards that aim, whether it is by improving sales or marketing or production, or whatever else is needed. Yes, they may have been good at playing the instrument, but now they need to conduct the whole orchestra. You have to trust your team to do the job.

There is nothing wrong with being in the detail – far from it. You just need to be in the right detail. Returning to cars for the moment, a car dashboard is perhaps a useful way of explaining how far we all need to get into the detail. Dashboards are designed to give you the precise amount of information you need to drive your car. They tell you how fast you are going, the amount of fuel you have and so on. They don't overload you with information. There is no need to tell you that your tyre pressure is X psi or that the amount of water in your windscreen washers is Y litres. The only time you need to know this detail is if the amounts are outside the required limits or indicate a looming problem. No one would want vehicle designers to shrink down the windscreen so they could put in a larger dashboard to take in every possible piece of information about the workings of a car. It would be distracting and impossible to manage. Yet, oddly, there are many organisations that are set up so the leader can do just this. They have the equivalent of large dashboards, showing all the KPIs (key performance indicators) that they possibly can. Does any leader ever need this level of detail? Of course not. In fact, it becomes an unnecessary distraction. All any leader needs is to encourage a culture where a member of the team can come forward when the equivalent of the tyre pressure gets low, to say: *something is wrong. We need to do something about it.* Leaders don't need all of the detail all of the time. They just need a process where someone is able to come forward and alert them. That is the moment they need to swoop down into the detail and take appropriate action.

ZOOMING IN AND OUT

A question that I occasionally get asked is whether the balance between the big picture and being in the detail is based on a divide between the leader and their team. In other words, should the leader mainly just think the lofty big-picture thoughts and then enable their team to get on with things by tackling the detail? While it is a key role of a leader to constantly remind everyone of the big picture, or 'this is where we are going', they are not the sole keeper of the big picture. The balance to be had here is not based on a case of divide and rule, where the leader comes up with the big-picture vision statement and everyone below that level works out the detail. There is plenty of scope to work together on the big picture. In fact, if the team is involved in creating the vision, they are far more likely to buy into it and therefore deliver it. It should be said though, of course, that the person at the top is always the one who bears the responsibility.

Likewise, when it comes to the detail, while everyone on the team needs to be focused on their goals and individual roles in addressing the detail, the person at the top of the organisation is in the unique position of being able to constantly look left and right to weigh up upcoming threats and opportunities, just as I found in the olive grove anecdote that opened this book. These details are the connecting points between what the team is doing, who they are doing it for and developments in the wider world. If this balance is not managed effectively, the results can be catastrophic.

For any leader, the balance between the big picture and being in the detail requires mental agility. Certainly, in my observation, the most successful leaders are those who relentlessly focus on the big picture but, when required, will zoom into the detail, request any required adjustments are made, and then zoom out again. It's not an easy thing to do and requires some degree of brain power and focus, and also the confidence to delegate and zoom out.

Someone who really managed to achieve this big-picture versus zooming-into-the-detail balance very well indeed was British cycling performance director Dave Brailsford, who was behind Team Sky's meteoric rise to success in cycling. Launched in 2010, the team's declared ambition was to win the Tour de France with a British rider within five years. They did it too. In fact, Bradley Wiggins achieved the goal in two.

The entirely single-minded approach was the brainchild of

Brailsford, who would often say something like 'Unless what you are doing is something towards this goal, you should not be doing it' – which is very similar to the British rowing team's philosophy that opened this chapter. Brailsford built a strategy on the back of this goal, which was all about the all-important marginal gains required to get there. The marginal gains – the how – were the real detail. They were the nuts and bolts of improving performance. You can't have one without the other. You can't decide on the detail and how to get there unless you have a clear goal. If you are all about the detail, no one knows what they are working towards.

What is important here is that Brailsford did not need to be there for every element of the detail. He didn't need to hang out in the cycle factories, supervising the making of every link in every bicycle chain. He didn't need to be in the kitchens, making sure the nutritionists put in the correct amounts of carbs and protein to help the cyclists achieve the optimum physique. Brailsford's aim was to make sure everyone knew the big picture. When required, if something was not going to plan, he would zoom right in and ask the question: *what is this doing towards the five-year goal? How does this move us forward?* He could then, just as easily, extract himself and move on to the next thing. The danger for any leader arises if they zoom in and then stay there, becoming obsessed with an aspect of the minutiae, failing to recognise that anything else is going on around them or to focus on the big picture.

QUESTIONS

To help judge your natural inclination on a scale between centralised control and delegation *see* Table 5. Decide where you sit on each spectrum, where 1 means you strongly agree with the first statement, 2 means you somewhat agree with the first statement, 3 means you agree with each statement about equally, 4 means you somewhat agree with the second statement and 5 means you strongly agree with the second statement. There are no wrong answers – this is simply a guide to help you reflect and perhaps adjust where required.

	1	2	3	4	5	
I prefer to focus on the big picture not the detail	1	2	3	4	5	I prefer to focus on the detail rather than the big picture
I believe the primary function of leadership is about creating visions that people find inspiring	1	2	3	4	5	I believe that the primary function of leadership requires you to know what is going on in the organisation.
I have never been told that I am getting 'into the weeds' too much	1	2	3	4	5	I frequently get told that I am 'in the weeds' too much
I have been guilty of not knowing enough about what my team are working on	1	2	3	4	5	I always know what my team are working on
I need to 'step in' more	1	2	3	4	5	I need to 'step out' more

Table 5. Big Picture and In the Detail

CHAPTER SEVEN
EMPATHETIC — DETACHED

The 2011 movie *Moneyball* was based on the bestselling book by Michael Lewis about Billy Beane's pioneering use of data analytics in major league baseball. In one scene, Beane (played by Brad Pitt), the general manager of Oakland Athletics, is instructing his assistant general manager, Peter Brand (Jonah Hill), on how to let a player know he's been cut from the team, traded with another club or sent down to the minor leagues. Beane wants to see how Brand will get along breaking the bad news and asks Brand to pretend that he's telling him that he's been cut from the team. What follows is a toe-curlingly uncomfortable explanation as Brand talks around the houses to explain to Beane why he has been cut. Along the way, Brand outlines the full complexities of the situation and gives a detailed description of his own emotional distress about being in the awful position of letting his man go. Luckily, we only get about half way through this painful exercise before Beane steps in and abruptly cuts off his assistant. 'Stop it,' he commands. 'Just deliver the news straight. Billy, you've been cut from the team. I am sorry it didn't work out – here's a phone number for you to call to handle the details.'

Now, there may be a school of thought that says Beane's

approach is harsh, even callous. After all, for the person being fired or demoted, the decision is so much more personal than just business. Most people are, after all, intensely reliant on their job to earn a living. Suddenly finding out that you are losing your main source of income is a shocking and stressful experience. And that's before you even get to the very real impact it can have on your confidence to be told, somewhat bluntly, that you just weren't up to the job. The truth is, though, that while empathy is usually exactly the right characteristic to show when tough messages need to be delivered, it is entirely wrong to beat about the bush. Deliver the bad news cleanly and directly, while at the same time showing some understanding of the difficult nature of the conversation. Beane's approach is detached, even brutal, but entirely correct in the circumstances. He needs to be direct and stick to the facts. While empathy is required, there is no room for too much empathy at a time like this. No one is going to thank you for weeping along with them. And that is probably doubly so in the *Moneyball* example. Major league professional athletes, who earn millions of dollars a year like the characters in the film, will be familiar with the volatile, cut-throat nature of sporting clubs. They'll also be fairly sure of picking up another good position pretty quickly.

There is a natural human tendency to try to display empathy when delivering bad news, because we can't help but think about how we'd feel, but softening the message won't change it. All any such attempts will do is get the person delivering the message into trouble. The recipient of the kind words will be confused and angry. *But you said I am doing a great job and have made a tremendous contribution – why are you firing me?* They may even turn any attempts to be empathetic against the person who is doing their best to be encouraging. It's the sort of thing that could tie your HR department up in knots for months to come and turn into a very costly mistake indeed.

Fortunately, the process of detachment is often built into the hierarchy of a business. Most chief executives will know their executive team very well but will naturally be a little more detached from those further down the organisation. After all, there are only so many people that it is possible to get to know well on a one-to-one basis. This structure can be helpful when the tough decisions need to be executed. Chief executives who know that they tend to err on the side of being empathetic can deal with the occasional need to be detached by leaning heavily on a kind of 'good cop, bad cop' routine. Here, the financial director generally assumes the bad cop role, delivering the tough blows, leaving the chief executive to deal with team morale. This partnership only works well if both parties are in agreement, and it can take a toll in the long term as anyone who is constantly seen to be detached will get a reputation for being cold.

DETACHED, BUT NOT TOO DETACHED

Anyone in a leadership position who sticks doggedly to the tough line, come what may, will risk harming long-term relationships and will inevitably lose the loyalty of the team. Imagine, for example, that a member of the team approaches a highly detached leader and quietly explains that they have personal issues. Perhaps they need some time off to deal with a medical problem, or maybe a member of their family requires support. If the leader turns this request down flat because they are only concerned with the smooth running of their organisation and can't see anything beyond that, it will inevitably alienate the person who asked for help. It's quite likely that there will be a knock-on effect on their colleagues too, who will see the very obvious unfairness in this singled-minded, seemingly off-hand approach. I have seen this exact scenario in a number of finance companies. The leadership in top City firms is often fiercely intelligent, which they need to be in order to succeed at the demanding job. However, they struggle to deal with the emotional, more caring side of leadership and that can drag a team down.

Detached leadership can very quickly devolve into something far more sinister and even ultimately destructive if it descends to the level of bullying. The fast-paced world of finance, referenced above, is a case in point. In Chapter Two, we looked at the case of Fred Goodwin, or 'Fred the Shred', who would brutally quiz his Royal Bank of Scotland senior managers each day at 9.30, openly questioning their worth.[15] And there have been plenty of other finance chiefs whose go-to tactic when it comes to staff management has been extreme intimidation. Indeed, there is no doubt that one of the contributing factors to the 2008/9 global financial crisis was the bullying, profit-at-all-costs culture at many leading financial organisations. Take

---

15 Ian Fraser, *Shredded: Inside RBS, the Bank that Broke Britain* (New York: Birlinn, 2014).

Lehman Brothers, which subsequently collapsed in the downturn. Dick Fuld, the former chief executive, was not shy in making his expectations known. At one Lehman's conference, when it was discovered that Lehman's stock was under attack, he declared that he wanted to find the short seller and 'tear his heart out and eat it before his eyes while he's still alive'.[16] No one was under any illusions about how far this leader was prepared to go to achieve his goals. Touchy-feely management this was not. (Although it could be argued that Fuld was passionate – it was just that he was passionate about the numbers above all other considerations.)

Today, with the benefit of hindsight, we know much more about the consequences of constant bullying and intimidation in the workplace in the run up to the financial crisis. Bankers, desperate not to be singled out or unfairly judged, cut corners, or, worse still, came up with all sorts of highly complex, yet entirely questionable, financial instruments to achieve the goals they were set. The problem is, if you don't care about how people do things, they will always get you the results that you seek. Somehow. However, it's also inevitable that the behaviour will eventually blow up in everyone's faces. This is exactly what happened and, in this instance, the results of the behaviour took the world's economy with it and condemned billions to years of austerity in the aftermath. When detached leadership is the default approach, it is inevitable that risks will be taken and mistakes will be made.

---

16 Stefan Stern, 'Bully-boy school of management' (*Financial Times*, 4 May 2009), https://www.ft.com/content/4aecb04a-38c4-11de-8cfe-00144feabdc0.

THE RIGHT DEGREE OF EMPATHY

You can't lead people unless you can put yourself in their shoes and understand how they are feeling. This is what builds that connection between the leader and their team. It's the under-standing that both sides 'get it' and have each other's backs. While empathy is often dismissed as a bit of a touchy-feely skill, it does have a major impact on leadership. Any leader who is completely devoid of empathy won't be able to build understanding, which is an important part of the relationship. Instead of being seen as someone who is working alongside their team, with the team's best interests at heart as well as the best interests of the organisation as a whole, the leader will come across as a tough, self-obsessed taskmaster. I don't know many people who want to work with someone like that, and if they do it is unlikely they'll give them their all.

Empathy is a two-way street too. It's not all about putting that metaphorical arm around people's shoulders and checking they are okay. If that bond is there, it means people are more willing to open up. If they know they're being listened to, they'll speak the truth to power. That sort of insight is invalua-ble for gaining the complete picture of what is going on, which is, of course, vital for balanced leadership.

We talked earlier about how crucial detachment is when making tough calls, such as reducing headcount, and how any-one making these calls needs to steer clear of seeming overly empathetic. However, it is important to be flexible according to the wider context of each specific scenario. There is a need for some significant empathy for those who are left behind after a reduction in headcount, whether it is one person or hundreds. I have several times witnessed just how disruptive restructuring can be. You too may have seen how, if handled badly, an exercise like this can lead to the loss of some very good people over and above the allotted redundancies. Even if you haven't, think about how disturbing the chain of events can be. At times like this, it is not unusual for a huge amount of noise to be made about the job cull itself, which organisations try to spin into a positive by making lots of grand announcements about the present and future. The hubbub of these announcements generally shuts down almost instantly after the last fired executive leaves the building. *All done now – nothing to see here.* However, if the senior team hasn't taken the time to listen to the people who are staying on and put themselves in their place, it is inevitable that a huge amount of imbalance will ensue. The whole process will have been deeply unsettling and now the entire dynamic in the organisation will have changed. It's painful too, when people say goodbye to colleagues and are themselves wrenched out of their positions and asked to work in an entirely different environment to shore up the gaps. This process needs to be handled with sensitivity and empathy, and that will take time (for planning) and effort if an organisation wants to retain the people it has decided to keep on after a redundancy programme. Get it wrong and that won't happen.

And it's not just that the good people will leave as soon as they can, either. There may well be a huge drop in performance among those who chose to stay. In one case I experienced, the process was handled so badly that one senior member of the team, who was supposed to be staying on and leading the restructuring, got into such a flap about everything that they were next to useless. It had a knock-on impact on the rest of the team, because they all lost respect for this person, who clearly was not coping well. As a result, the entire process was even worse than it might have been. A bit of empathy and understanding early on would have resulted in a completely different outcome.

One of the biggest dangers with trying to show empathy arises when it doesn't come naturally. If it is forced, it can seem inauthentic. This inauthenticity will stand out a mile; team members will inevitably put two and two together and decide that the boss is only being nice to them because they want something or are about to deliver bad news. The bullshit alarm will go off and it won't matter if the team members are mistaken and making 5 out of their 2 + 2 calculation; even if the boss genuinely has their best interests at heart, the imbalance will be there. They'll be wary and on their guard, and that is not an environment that's conducive to good work.

Even if this inauthenticity somehow fools everyone, it will unravel. I once worked with a director who by nature was very direct and controlling, yet he did his best to mask this by appearing to be very empathetic. He kept things very much to himself, not telling people what was going on, but he framed this behaviour as him wanting to 'protect' people and keep the stress on his own shoulders. In reality, he just didn't like to be questioned about some of the decisions he was making, or be challenged in any way. This all completely unravelled when this person moved on to another job in another company. His successor arrived to find all sorts of skeletons tucked away in closets. While this character had seemed perfectly balanced, he was in fact operating completely out of balance and the results of his actions (or inactions) reverberated through the organisation for years afterwards.

It's not the easy option to display empathy, and it can be demanding to maintain on a daily basis because it requires patience. It takes time to listen, show awareness and display the understanding required. Often it means putting people ahead of yourself, because that is what is required to earn the team's trust. It is not, however, good leadership to be too empathetic, all the time. Alarm bells always ring for me when I consult with a business and everyone I speak to internally tells me what a lovely organisation it is to work for.

'It's just such a nice place to be,' they'll say. 'Easily the best place I've ever worked.'

This is a prime indicator of a surfeit of empathy.

'What are your challenges?' I will probe when I uncover an organisation like this. 'How often do you have feedback conversations with your managers?'

I invariably find that people who work in an overly empathetic environment can't think of any particularly difficult challenges and, as for feedback, it rarely happens. Not on a formal basis anyhow and, whenever anything is said about performance, it is simply to praise everyone for doing a great job. Of course, this is all fantastic during the good times and who wouldn't like to work for a business like this? But, and this is key, what happens when an organisation that operates like this goes through a bad patch?

This is exactly what happened to one organisation I worked with that had a very obvious excess of empathy. When the business hit the buffers and headcount needed to be cut, it was catastrophic. The managers were completely unprepared to have the difficult conversations and some even refused to take part. The people who were cut were shocked and saddened. Since they had never had any feedback, they all felt that they were doing a brilliant job and were utterly essential to the organisation. Even those who survived the cull were left demoralised and utterly broken. It was a horrendous exercise for everyone and a really, really tough job to rebuild what was left of the organisation. None of this is to say exercises like this are *easy* for a more balanced organisation, but they are definitely *easier*. People don't like it, but they are more willing to have the hard conversations and get things done.

Even if you are not looking at extreme circumstances such as redundancy, a surfeit of empathy can cause paralysis on a day-to-day basis. The action, or perhaps inaction, of an overly empathetic leader will help to put the entire team in its comfort zone (*see* Chapter Four) and keep them there. Individuals will never seek out anything challenging or try anything new to push the business forward. Why would they? The boss is happy with what they are doing as it stands. You might equate this scenario with the hotly debated modern system of educating and parenting, which rewards *participation* in events rather than *achievements*. A gold star for everyone! Yes, it's empathetic and great for a kid's personal esteem, but I am never entirely sure it helps young people move towards living in the real world. It doesn't force them to strive for something better.

As Roderic says, one of his most valuable lessons as a child was playing tennis with his stepfather. The adult said from the get-go that he would not pander to Roderic's youth or inexperience and would always play to his full ability. That way, he said, when Roderic did eventually win, he would value it more. To date, Roderic still hasn't done so, even though his stepfather is now 72, but he says he could now probably give him a run for his money! All joking aside, this approach may not be particularly empathetic, but it encourages maximum effort and means that, when an achievement is (finally) made, it is really, really valued.

YOU ARE NOT EVERYONE'S BEST FRIEND

Any leader who is aware that they tend towards being overly empathetic needs to address the situation. If they don't, it will stop them from making the tough decisions that need to be made because they will be too concerned about the impact on others. An excess of empathy holds leaders back and is corrosive to the organisation they lead. Imagine, for example, the case of a company employing 100,000 people in an economic downturn. In these circumstances, it might emerge that the best thing for the company's future is to reduce headcount by 20,000. Doing so will save the jobs of the other 80,000. If the boss is too empathetic, they will dither and delay on making this crucial decision. In the worst-case scenario, hesitating for too long could mean it becomes too late for everyone.

On a purely personal basis, being too empathetic can have

a very detrimental effect on a leader themselves too. One of my consultancy assignments was with a partner in a law firm who was at the end of her tether and completely wrung out by work. It didn't take long to get to the nub of the problem. It isn't unusual for legal teams to have to pull all-nighters when big cases and transactions get to a crucial juncture. In this case, though, she'd constantly been unwilling to ask her associates and trainees to stay behind to help out.

'Invariably, they'll have told me about their plans for the evening and I haven't got the heart to ask them to kill them,' she said.

As a result, thanks to this excess of empathy, this partner shouldered the entire workload and was getting more and more exhausted. Her work was suffering because of it and important transactions were getting delayed. Meanwhile, her family life was suffering too, because she was always the one to stay late.

Achieving the balance between empathy and detachment means that you won't always be everyone's best friend. You can't be. A good starting point in the scenario described here is to remind yourself of the adage I mentioned before: don't ever do something when someone who is paid less than you can do it. It sounds harsh, but that is how it works. They have their job and you have yours. When they do their job, it leaves you to do yours properly. You are not there to do the work for your team. You are there to provide them with all the things that they need to do the job they are employed to do. But they need to do the job. Equally, don't second-guess what they will feel about being asked to do the job they are being paid to do. If they are committed to their job, they won't think twice about completing their allotted tasks.

The profession of a surgeon provides many useful clues on how to get the balance right here. This group of people, in particular, are required to work at both ends of the scale when it comes to empathy and detachment. When operating on a patient, they need to be detached. This is because they need to take a single-minded approach to the job. They can't let emotion cloud their judgement or distract them. However, later, when they leave the operating theatre to speak with relatives, their empathy must come to the fore – particularly if the prognosis is not as good as hoped. Arguably, the time when things go most wrong is when they don't get the empathy part right. Most people will accept that surgery is not an exact science. Things can, and do, go wrong. However, if a doctor promises too much and delivers little, or, at the other end of the scale, is rude and dismissive, that is when families start to ring lawyers.

Other clues on getting this balance right can be gained from the military, which provides us with an intense example that involves both extremes (empathy and detachment) at the same time. In the armed forces, it is crucial to build a relationship based on mutual trust and respect among everyone in a unit, and this is only achieved through empathy and support. Equally, commanders know that they may well have to ask the people in their charge to do a job that will get them killed, which requires a huge act of detachment. A classic illustration of this occurs in a firefight. Although the troop or platoon will know that the enemy is out there, they won't always know exactly where they are. To find out, someone has to be asked to do something called 'break cover'. It's exactly as it sounds, meaning this soul has to break cover and then run like hell while people shoot at them. The objective is to show where the enemy is hidden, so they can be dealt with. Of course, this involves someone in the squad being asked to put themselves in considerable harm's way. The commander can't shy away from making this request or be too empathetic about their people at that particular moment in time. If they are, they are not going to be able to get everyone out of the situation. The very best they can do at that intense moment is to balance the request by reassuring the individual who has been selected to break cover that they will be supported by the rest of the team, or by an air strike being called in. Because the leader has spent months and years building a relationship with their people, through fairness, empathy and support, everyone will trust that this is going to happen.

In a business setting, achieving the right balance involves creating a place where individuals recognise and appreciate the empathy of those in charge and feel that the organisation is a nice place to work, but at the same time also feel challenged. Leaders should steer clear of being known for a one-size-fits-all approach where they pride themselves on their directness or, at the other end of the spectrum, their ability to always listen and understand. Individuals don't want, or need, consistency. They need the person in charge to react appropriately according to the situation. They'll be challenged when they need to be challenged, but listened to when they've got something important to say.

When Roderic and I do workshops, we often do an exercise where we ask groups to discuss the characteristics of the best and worst leaders they ever worked with. We end up with a long list of leadership buzzwords, such as decisive, challenging or empathetic, but what is most interesting is the stories behind those words. Invariably, the bosses who seem to come out on top are quite tough taskmasters. They expect their teams to deliver and they challenge them if they don't. And the teams don't mind demanding bosses with high standards – clearly so, since they rate them as the best leaders. However, these individuals also need to know that, on the odd occasion, if something did happen and they needed a more empathetic stance from their boss, they would get it.

Whatever happens, getting the balance of detachment and empathy right will always be demanding for leaders. I'll reference another movie here that illustrates this perfectly. The film in question is *The Imitation Game*, which tells the story of the mathematician, code-breaker and computer pioneer Alan Turing (Benedict Cumberbatch), who broke the Enigma code and changed the course of the Second World War. Once the Enigma code has been cracked and intelligence starts to come in about imminent German attacks, one of the principal characters, Peter Hilton (Matthew Beard), realises that his brother is serving on a ship that is about to be targeted. A tense scene follows where Turing argues strongly that they cannot warn Hilton's brother, since to do so would alert the enemy that they'd broken the Enigma code and therefore endanger countless more lives. Turing's response is detached. The team has to think of the bigger picture, which is to win the war. Even so, this real-life decision has to have been one of the toughest choices to make, involving crushing all empathetic thoughts altogether.

QUESTIONS

To help judge your natural inclination on a scale between centralised control and delegation *see* Table 6 on the opposite page. Decide where you sit on each spectrum, where 1 means you strongly agree with the first statement, 2 means you somewhat agree with the first statement, 3 means you agree with each statement about equally, 4 means you somewhat agree with the second statement and 5 means you strongly agree with the second statement. There are no wrong answers – this is simply a guide to help you reflect and perhaps adjust where required.

	1	2	3	4	5	
I think leaders need to be good friends with their team members	1	2	3	4	5	I think that leaders need to be approachable but not good friends with their team members
I find it hard to make tough decisions if they negatively impact the lives of people	1	2	3	4	5	I have no issues making tough decisions that can/could negatively impact the lives of people
I would find it very hard to make people redundant	1	2	3	4	5	I would not find it hard to make people redundant
Team members seem to be comfortable sharing personal challenges with me	1	2	3	4	5	Team members rarely share personal challenges with me
I know my team very well	1	2	3	4	5	I don't know my team very well

Table 6. Empathetic and Detached

PART TWO

SKILLS TO PERFECT THE RIGHT BALANCE EVERY TIME

CHAPTER EIGHT
JUDGEMENT AND CONTEXT

If you accept the premise that leadership is about getting things done both with and through others, the natural extension is that a leader's role is to make the right judgement between when to take the lead themselves and when to release control to the team. The ability to continuously assess and understand new circumstances, in order to make this choice over and over again, will largely determine the success or failure of any organisation. As we've seen, circumstances constantly change and so do the behaviours that are needed to deal with those changing circumstances. To achieve the right balance, the skill that every leader needs to perfect is the ability to judge the right approach to use at a given moment. This requires rapid, but careful, weighing up of the information required to make wise decisions that produce the desired outcomes.

Judgement relies on a complete understanding of the context of a situation. Without knowing the context, it is impossible to make a call about the best place to land on the relevant balance spectrum (*see* Part One) – the place where a leader is most effective. How, then, should we define context? What are the elements that are required to understand it in any situation? At the most basic level, there are a number of elements to consider:

- *Historical context*. What has been the situation up to now, leading up to this current position?

- *Strategic context.* Context varies in accordance with the strategic picture or end goal. This is the same for a specific project as it is for the big-picture vision of an organisation as a whole.

- *Human context.* If an individual is involved, what is the context around that individual and what part do they play in it? Also, what is the character of that individual? Some people respond positively to a well-timed motivational push in the right direction, while others just need to be told what needs to be done.

- *Team context.* If a team is involved, do you need to treat them as one body or take account of the individuals within the team? Also, how do you treat everyone fairly but equally as individuals?

Once the context is better understood, it is much easier to use judgement about how to respond to a situation and work out the best way of behaving.

Roderic has an interesting example of this, which he says taught him the most about judgement in leadership even though it happened in the domestic setting of his home. His very young daughter had woken in the middle of the night and was very agitated and upset. Roderic's reaction was to go into her room, remonstrate with her, and basically tell her to go back to bed and get to sleep. It was, he admits, not his most motivational or soothing speech, but it was the result of many months of sleep deprivation of the kind that most parents of very young children will entirely relate to. As he quickly discovered, though, his somewhat brisk approach had the opposite effect from what he intended, causing the little girl to cry even more. At this point, Roderic's wife intervened. She had been listening to the unfolding situation from the room next door. She walked in, quietly picked up the toddler and gently stroked her hair. Their daughter was immediately soothed and the crisis was averted. To Roderic, this was the most powerful lesson of leadership he had seen to date, including all his time spent in the Marines. In his view, his wife immediately summed up the context and used her judgement to choose a way of behaving that got the best outcome out of that situation. Making a behaviour judgement in any circumstances, whether at home or at work, might mean changing your natural leadership style to fit with whatever is the most effective option.

THE ESTIMATE PROCESS

For a leader, improving their judgement is an important skill that they should learn at the earliest possible moment in their career, so it quickly becomes an ingrained habit. One of the things that the military is very, very good at is developing a thought process in its leaders that enables them to quickly analyse any situation that they find themselves in. The technique is called the Estimate Process and it's a tool that enables leaders to ask some very basic questions in the heat of the moment to get to the nub of the context quickly and cleanly. An abridged version of those questions is:

- What's happening?
- Why is that happening?

- What am I being asked to do?
- What are the tools that I have available to me?

I can attest to the fact that when you begin to learn this process, it feels very strange indeed. I still vividly remember being forced into trying it in all sorts of active situations during my training at Sandhurst and at first it felt very unnatural. Yet, by the end of my training, I found myself doing it instinctively. Something would happen and *boom*, I would deal with the immediate issue, but then I would pause, get my map out, gather my team around me and create a forced pause so I could gain clarity. This was my cue to take a breather and then run through the series of Estimate Process analyses that needed to be done. Even today, I automatically apply it to almost any situation I find myself in.

Right at the beginning of the book, I mentioned that both Roderic and I have found ourselves first on the scene at road traffic accidents. I am pretty sure we both followed the Estimate Process to a tee. I didn't even notice myself doing it at the time, but on reflection I realise that I immediately began to scroll through the questions in my head. What had happened? Why was it happening? What was I being asked to do? What were the tools I had to deal with it? It was ingrained.

Obviously, not everyone will have the benefit of training at Sandhurst, but all leaders need to work at developing the skill of taking a step back to sum up a situation. If you wish to become effective at managing the spectrums outlined in Part One, this is the starting point each time. Pause, take 30 seconds and work out what is needed.

It is quite rare to find someone who naturally does this without thinking twice about it. Some people even go into total flap mode. It takes a real leader to come along and say, *stop flapping, let's calm down for a second.* In the old days we used to call it a 'Hamlet moment' after an advertising campaign for Hamlet cigars that ran from the mid-sixties until 1991, when tobacco advertising was finally banned from our TV screens. The ads featured a series of awkward and embarrassing moments, which are 'saved' when the lead character presses the pause button and lights up his cigar. The premise is that this makes him smile and forget his woes. This is not to encourage cigar smoking but merely to encourage you to find some mechanism to help you stop and run through the options. Soon it will become ingrained.

One of the best examples I've seen in a corporate setting of the effective use of this pause moment was via a young man I trained some years back. I will call him Simon. Simon was a super-keen new hire who was working on his first ever multi-million-pound deal. Somewhere along the way, he made the most horrendous mistake. He emailed a colleague to complain about someone on the client team who was, in his view, not pulling their weight. It was one of those half jokey, half serious but quite cheeky (well, let's be honest here, rude) emails. But, it didn't go to the colleague. He sent it to the client in question.

When he realised what he'd done, his initial reaction was predictably one of complete horror. It was a disaster in every way. Simon was convinced his firm was going to lose the deal and, as a result, he'd lose his job. After he'd managed to quell the initial wave of nausea, Simon trudged off to his boss's office to admit the screw-up and face the music.

You can only imagine what went through the mind of Simon's boss as he heard the story. Simon admitted that the client had responded with a curt 'you didn't mean to send that to me, did you?' email, but he suspected that the fall-out was brewing up to be much worse. Yet the boss's reaction was a textbook example of the Estimate Process. He invited Simon to take a seat and in the time that it took for the distraught young manager to settle into the office chair, the boss spoke calmly, basically saying, *hold on, let's take a moment to look at this more fully*. As he was saying these things, I have no doubt that the boss was running through all the implications and thinking about what to do next. What had happened? Why was it happening? What are the tools I have to deal with it? This pause was enough for him to understand the context and to begin formulating a plan. His approach of beginning by calming everything down was exactly the right one. After some judicious apologies, the day was saved and neither Simon nor the client parted company with his firm.

TAKE THE TEMPERATURE OF THE ROOM

As leaders become more experienced, they won't need to follow a complex process of slowing everything down to rethink. It will become an automatic reaction. They simply need the confidence to take the temperature of the room and shift perspective from worrying about what has happened to thinking about what needs to be done next to resolve it.

Roderic has another really good example, from his research into Sir Ernest Shackleton, who led the Imperial Trans-Atlantic Expedition to the Antarctic beginning in 1914. After three years, Shackleton and his 27-strong crew faced a terrible situation when their ship, the *Endurance*, was crushed by pack ice in the Weddell Sea off Antarctica. The entire crew had to abandon ship and faced an uncertain future as the wooden polar yacht collapsed in on itself and sank into 3,000 metres of water.

While the crew's story of escape across frozen floes and in lifeboats is extraordinary, what is most interesting in relation to judgement is the way Shackleton handled the moments around the initial unfolding of the disaster. He calmly made sure the entire crew got off the *Endurance* and then gathered them all together on the ice to watch the ship's final moments as it slipped beneath the freezing water. We can surmise that he did this to help shape the context of how the team were thinking. He needed them to pause as they let the reality of their situation bed in. Then, once the top end of the mast had disappeared, he said, 'Now we'll go home.'[17] It is exactly the same as the Estimate Process: this is what has happened, and now we are looking at how we will move forward.

Any person in a leadership position is, or at least should be, the best person to understand the context. They should be close enough to the action to understand all the elements that go into making the right decision. When I am training

17 Nancy F. Koehn, 'Leadership lessons from the Shackleton expedition' (*New York Times*, 24 December 2011), https://www.nytimes.com/2011/12/25/business/leadership-lessons-from-the-shackleton-expedition.html.

people in this, I often use a fictitious example of a young new commander, straight out of Sandhurst, in Afghanistan. A bomb goes off, virtually right in front of him. He gets on the phone to his commander and says, 'What should I do?' The entirely correct response from this commander is, 'It's up to you – make a decision.' This young commander is the only one on the ground who can take the real temperature of the situation and therefore make the decision about what to do next. He has eyes and ears on the complete picture. The senior commander is ten kilometres behind him. But, and this is key, the new commander will know that whatever decision he does make about what to do next, the senior command will be right behind him, backing him up.

The idea of being on the ground is not just a figurative way of viewing a situation either. There is no substitute for being close to the action. Sitting in your ivory tower, relying on second-hand reports or technology to feed you all the information, won't give you a full picture. As Roderic found from his time serving in Afghanistan, technology is not infallible. While military technology has improved immensely since he and I served, and there are now a number of feeds coming from various sources to alert the troops on the ground to potential threats, there is no substitute for the evidence of your own eyes. One time Roderic's platoon was given multiple warnings about a group of fighters in a compound, which he was told to clear. As it turned out, though, the compound was completely empty when they approached. The weight of technology, from several different sources, got it wrong. The advantage Roderic had at his fingertips was that he was there, on the ground. No operations room could tell what he could, from their position five kilometres away. The person on the ground is in the detail and can make their decisions on a better-informed basis.

Being close to the action (or keeping an eye on the big picture versus the detail) pays dividends in any organisation, but it is not a one-off thing. It has to become a habit because the context changes so frequently. Something will always be forcing an organisation off balance. It's not unlike a game of tennis. The player will try to take a position in the middle of the court on the baseline. It is their opponent's job to knock the ball all over the court, so the player has to run around and then return to their spot. Sooner or later they are going to make a mistake or not manage to get back to the ball in time. The same goes for a corporate setting; competitors will always be seeking to steal a march by undercutting your prices, offering a better delivery service or bringing out a better version of what you are selling. An issue with a supplier will have an impact on people in the team, or there may be a change in the sales environment that means more or fewer customers. These things all throw the organisation out of balance. Your job as a leader is to try to remain in balance.

OVERCOME THE FEAR OF THE UNKNOWN

While many leaders accept that they need to assess the context of each situation before making a judgement call, some people do struggle with the next stage: making the decision and acting upon it. They find it easier to stick with what they have always known, or how they usually react, rather than take a step into the unknown. I once worked with a chief executive of a company that had offices all over Europe and the Middle East. This person had recently been promoted from her post as head of UK sales, but she clearly found the scale of the top job pretty daunting.

'This is massive,' she said to me. 'I've got to do all my UK stuff, plus I need to get to know all the new territories. That's before you get into managing all the new teams.'

To me, this was a very clear case of this person wrapping herself in the comfort blanket of her well-worn UK territory. She knew all the processes and systems and enjoyed the familiarity of them. She was fearful of the challenges in France, Abu Dhabi and Finland, which seemed very different to the ones she was used to. In this new context, she would also most likely need to get to grips with a number of new techniques as well as learn all sorts of unfamiliar processes. It was clear to me that she not only needed to understand the new context she was operating in but also embrace it.

The way I helped her work through the new challenge was to encourage her to break the issue down. We all have a certain amount of capacity. Our work day (and indeed our personal life too) is dominated by a to-do list (whether written down or in our heads), which contains all the tasks that we need to finish to fulfil our job as well as everyone's expectations and demands of us. The new chief executive was attempting to pour an entire bucket of new tasks on top of the list that she'd been managing for years.

I had to be blunt with her.

'You have to realise that you can't do it all,' I told her.

'It is impossible to be in control of everything. You have to fundamentally rebalance yourself. Throw everything up into the air, take a look at it all and say to yourself: what do I need to do most and what can others do?'

In other words, she had to go through the equivalent of the Estimate Process in order to work out what was required in the new context, unload some of the bits from her original list and delegate those bits to others. She also had to take a good look at all the territories she now headed and work out what she could hand over to others elsewhere. Then, once she had made her assessment, she needed to act without delay.

It's not an easy balance to achieve, going from a position of retaining almost full control to delegating key parts of your job. It can feel like a huge leap and the obvious fear is that you will let go of the wrong task, leaving it to someone who really can't do what needs to be done. This is, in part, why I encouraged the new chief executive to press the pause button, step back, reflect and reset. It was a similar situation to the one after the Grim Reaper exercise, when I threw down my kit and started to head straight to the trenches before Sergeant McPhilips stopped me and made me step back (*see* Chapter Two).

BE CONFIDENT

Something that can hold people back from making the right judgement is confidence, and I suspect that there was an element of this in the above case of the new chief executive. Like any skill, though, confidence can be developed. The majority of the people that Roderic and I coach have the skills to be successful, balanced leaders, but they often lack the confidence to enact them. It can really help if you have a great boss who can nurture those skills and convince you that you're really good at something, but not everyone has this advantage. Even if you don't, though, it does really help if you recognise that you may be under-confident and it might be holding you back. It is a great first step in addressing the problem and building upon skills you already have.

Roderic has an interesting way of tackling confidence-building based on the stretch and recovery technique, which will be discussed in more detail in Chapter Ten and involves working towards a big goal by taking small steps. He draws an analogy with the way people are helped to get over claustrophobia – the irrational, yet intense, fear of small spaces. One therapy involves taking the claustrophobic person to a lift. In any circumstance, getting into a tiny carriage like this would be a claustrophobic person's worst nightmare. So, the initial stage of the therapy is to ask whether they can simply stand a couple of metres away from the lift and look at it for a short period of time. In the next session, they are asked to get a little closer to the lift and in the next, closer still. By the fourth or fifth session, they may be asked to wave their hand inside the lift. By this stage, the previously terrifying concept will be just about manageable.

Eventually, if the therapy progresses well, the claustrophobic person will get into the lift. The idea is to push the person's mental and physical limits to their natural point, and then a bit beyond that, building up the challenge over a period of time. Each time the much-feared task becomes easier. The fact that the steps forward are incremental means that the process never becomes overwhelming.

One of the most common manifestations of a lack of confidence is a fear of public speaking. My advice to anyone with this concern is to follow the same incremental process. Ask yourself, are you happy speaking to a room of, say, three or four people? Now, how about eight or nine? Each time you feel you have reached your comfort zone, take it up to the next level. I've done this and I know it works. I am a relatively comfortable public speaker and am happy to get up in front of audiences of 500 people or so. Yet, I did pause for a moment when I was asked to deliver a talk to 1500 people at a conference in the US. I built up to it, though, and did it. In fact, I really enjoyed it. I was in my element. And now, I'd be happy to do it again. Now I think I could probably attempt 10,000 given half the chance.

ACT!

Building confidence is crucial for the stage that follows on from judgement: execution. By now, you will have judged the context and framed the issue that demanded the judgement call. You will also have started to align the team behind your proposed course of action, so everyone understands why it is important. Now, the decision needs to be followed through with action.

To give yourself added peace of mind at this critical juncture, it is useful to consider the Service Test, which is one that Roderic and I used in our days in the military. When faced with a challenging situation, we'd weigh up our decision against how our actions, or inactions, might play out if they hit the front page of the newspapers. How would the actions be judged if they became public information, and would they have an adverse reaction on the unit? Trust me, this gives decision making a different perspective and will test your confidence and resolve. Added to this, it is not just the front pages of newspapers you need to think about these days. A very poorly executed decision could easily end up on social media and, in a worst-case scenario, go viral. If, though, you still feel confident in your decision, *act*. There really is no need to delay, and any hesitation may mean you react too late and need to go through the entire process again.

While getting the balance right for all stages is crucial, as is execution, it is just as important to be confident enough to adjust along the way to keep things steady. Judgements are never black and white – there is never a 'right' decision and a 'wrong' decision. There are many stages in between, which means things may well change and a leader needs to be prepared to change with them.

When a decision doesn't seem to be having the desired effect, there will be a number of clues as to why. If, for example, the team resists when you try to mobilise them in the preparation phase, it could be because you were too focused on the end point and didn't successfully communicate the goal. If this is the case, you can correct the imbalance by going back and correcting the framing.

I am a great believer in listening to your gut on this one.

If you start to get a feeling in the pit of your stomach that something is not quite right, listen to it. If you weigh it up and something is not going as you expected, speak with the team, tell them that something has changed and find the right course.

What really helps here is to make sure you have truth-tellers around you and that the environment you've created is one where people are unafraid to speak truth to power. If you've surrounded yourself with 'yes men', you will never know whether people have truly bought into your strategy. This brings us back to the Johari Window (*see* Chapter One), which can help you to better understand your relationships with yourself and others. If a judgement call is going awry, you want people to feel emboldened to have an honest conversation. They can say: *we made that call, but some new information has come to light and we need to revisit the decision*. Likewise, a leader has to have the courage to be able to respond that they don't feel a change is necessary. They've heard the alternative view but are convinced the original decision stands.

We all need to be willing to acknowledge that we make mistakes and admit to them when we do. In the military, there is an acceptance that a decision made under fire is never perfect, but, providing it is made with the best intent, that is okay. Delaying a decision, or not making one at all, is a lot, lot worse. It certainly does not make a fast-developing situation safer.

CHAPTER NINE
TRUST AND RELATIONSHIPS

The basis of the model of employment that we were all brought up with has not changed a whole lot since the Industrial Revolution, or even before that. Prior to the opening of factories up and down the land, our forebears left their homes each day to tend the fields. Then, with the advent of manufacturing processes, they swapped their outdoor lives for indoor ones, tending giant machines. People still needed to leave their homes each day, though. Businesses could easily measure their workers' worth by the amount of time they were on the production line and the idea of exchanging our time for money became deeply ingrained. It became the model of how we made our living. We left home and did a set pattern of hours each day, or regular shifts, and it was a very easy model to manage.

Oddly, despite the recent great changes in the way we work thanks to technology and the knowledge economy, that long-held idea of exchanging time for money has endured. Until recently, with the abrupt change of working practices thanks to the coronavirus lockdowns, our worth was still measured by the time we put in. Or should that be the *visible* work time we put in? In other words, I mean the time we spent in the office. Part of the problem, and possibly the reason we stuck with the outmoded model for so long, is that most firms are sceptical about using a value model to measure performance.

Put simply, if the bosses couldn't see what everyone was doing, they never quite trusted that the job was being done. Another big aspect of the problem here is that time is easy to measure, but value less so.

Roderic had some experience of this while he worked at Urenco UK, a nuclear fuel company, which was going through a strained period with regulators. In order to rebuild trust with the regulators, Simon Bowen, the then managing director, invited them into the organisation so they could see 'warts and all' what was working and what wasn't. It was an entirely different approach from before, but it was designed to generate trust between a company and its key stakeholder by helping them focus on the value of what was being done.

Our suspicion is that there is a generational element in the reluctance to think differently too. It may be a little bit of a generalisation, but many chief executives and others in senior leadership positions are from the older generation, perhaps in their fifties or even early sixties. The formative years of people in this age group were not spent amid the technological revolution and therefore many developed a different – but firm – view of what work looks like. For this generation, work means a commute to a city, to a large office, where people do their allocated jobs and all work together as they have done for a very long time. This in turn has added to the false assumption that if people are not in the office, they are not working. Generally, this is an entirely erroneous assumption and, indeed, can be 180 degrees wrong. Roderic and I have both been in organisations where everyone was present and correct in the office but the productivity was very poor indeed. It doesn't help that the culture of presentism promotes an atmosphere where everyone has to be seen to be busy, which often means asking other departments to undertake completely worthless tasks.

Roderic recalls working with one manufacturer where a team in the procurement department was charged with producing regular, detailed reports. However, when the reports were tracked, it revealed that no one at all was reading them! I don't think that this sort of thing will be a surprise to many, but rather a disappointing reality that is all too common.

As we saw during the coronavirus pandemic, people have now proved that they can work very effectively from home. The technology is there and many firms made very good use of it. There are clear opportunities here to build upon the model that evolved naturally (although very swiftly) during the pandemic and to cut teams a bit more slack. A little trust and flexibility go a long way. Bums on seats are not what is important; getting the task done is.

Imagine, for example, if an individual on the team has something they urgently needed to deal with outside work, perhaps to do with childcare or an issue with their car. The attitude in times gone by would have been: *sort it out on your own time – we need you in the office*. Today, it is much more effective to say: *take some time – get it sorted*. With support, that individual can go and resolve their problem and then return to do their work at a slightly later time. Chances are, they will go on to deliver significant value because their leadership has trusted them and given them space. That's 100% a good use of everyone's time and abilities. Leaders should always remember that they lead individuals and need to make time for those conversations.

Trust and relationships underpin all of the balance spectrums outlined in Part One. Any leader who does not have the trust and support of their team will struggle to adjust their style according to the context or the prevailing pressures. Balanced leadership is not something that can be achieved alone. The feedback, cooperation and understanding of others are crucial to success.

GETTING TO KNOW YOU

The ability to build relationships is a skill that we learn from a very young age. This is partly why there was so much concern about school closures during the first coronavirus lockdown in the UK. Children in early years classes were not just missing out on key parts of their education, where they begin to learn to read, write and understand basic maths; they were also skipping a crucial moment in their social development. These are the years when we learn how to form relationships with others, perfect the art of sharing, master give and take, and understand how to engage others. This period represents our first, crucial steps to building a fully functioning social network.

The natural assumption might be that the whole relationship-building thing is behind us by the time we reach adulthood – a tick in the box, another skill perfected. As we all know very well, though, that is not the case. Some people are far better at building and maintaining strong relationships than others. Those others apparently see very little value in putting in the time to foster these connections and as a result often seem aloof and detached. You may well recognise the workplace scenario where an individual bases their relationship approach on a series of assumptions about others, rather than taking the time to build a meaningful connection. They may, for example, assume a person's character from their job title, which then dictates how they engage with them. This is clearly a ridiculous assumption. The fact that someone is, say, head of marketing tells you pretty much nothing about the individual behind that title other than the fact that they may have a university education and might have studied marketing. Treating the current head of marketing in exactly the same way as the previous head of marketing and the one before that won't get you very far. If you want to have a meaningful and productive working relationship, you need to find out what makes each particular individual tick.

Be aware that in our professional and private lives, we all, at least to some degree, use an unconscious selection procedure when it comes to trust, whether or not we are predisposed to be quite trusting. At the extreme, think of meeting someone new who is dressed in jeans and a vest and has a prominent job-stopping face tattoo. Depending on your personal beliefs, this could be a signal not to trust the individual.

Of course, the reason why some individuals tend to generalise is because it is much easier to pigeonhole people with the shorthand clue of their job title. It requires more time and effort to get underneath the surface and find out about anyone's real motivations and aspirations. Nevertheless, I would still argue very strongly that it is time well spent. During our military training, both Roderic and I were told time and again that we needed to *know* our men. The mantra was that we needed to know them better than their own mothers knew them. If you ignore this crucial stage of leadership, the underlying message is that you don't care about the people you lead. If you are not even remotely curious about what motivates people under your charge, why they chose their particular career or where they see themselves in the future, why should they give you their all? And, of course, in the military, we need people to be prepared to give their all.

As a result of our training, we are both very attuned to the importance of the getting-to-know-you process and can describe times where we have seen it done really well, both in the military and in the corporate world.

Roderic cites an example of this being done very well by Major General Charles Stickland, who was a senior Royal Marines officer at the time and was later promoted all the way to the top, becoming Commandant General Royal Marines from January 2018 until June 2019. When he was the commanding officer of 42 Commando, a unit within the Royal Marines, every new officer who joined would be invited over to his house for a cup of tea and a conversation. He would ask the officer where they grew up, where they went to school and university, what they did there and what they enjoyed. He'd ask them about their previous units and what they'd experienced. It was not a dispassionate barrage of questions, either, but done in a friendly, affable manner. He also took the opportunity to explain a little about what he expected from his officers and his own philosophy of leadership. This was one of the most inspirational moments in Roderic's career, and he remembers it well even now, years later. There he was, second in command and not yet particularly senior, but the major general took more than an hour of his time to find out all about him.

Roderic saw a variation of this powerful technique used when he joined the nuclear industry after leaving the services. This time it was under the auspices of Gregory Smith, the chairman of the aforementioned Urenco UK, who had a slightly different approach that was no less effective. In this case, Smith, recently appointed as chairman, stood up at a town-hall-style address to the entire company and explained that he was giving the team what he described as 'a roadmap to me'. He came across as honest and approachable as he described his background and some of the key decisions he had made during the course of his career. He explained why he had decided to join the organisation and what he was excited about. If anyone on the team wanted to influence his thinking, he explained, they should tell him about what they wanted to do and explain why it was going to have an impact.

'Don't try and change my mind with figures,' he warned. 'I'm not a particularly numerate individual. I want to know about the human impact.'

In being frank about where his weaknesses lay, he invited the team to hold him to account in improving his own shortcomings and also to play to his strengths. At the end of the meeting, he announced that he would be holding a similar exercise with everyone in the company. He invited Roderic and all of his colleagues to provide their own roadmaps to them as individuals. Smith finished the town hall with one question: 'How do I help you to become more successful?'

As strategies for high-impact leadership, the approaches by Charles Stickland and Gregory Smith were unbelievable in their effect. As Roderic says, he would subsequently have 'walked through the gates of hell' for either leader. All of that from less than 90 minutes of conversation or speaking apiece. It seems to me that this kind of approach has to be a worthy investment in time for any leader. A relationship as solid as the two described here is a pretty strong foundation for success.

A big part of the reason why this getting-to-know-you technique is so successful goes back to the Johari Window, highlighted in Chapter One. A leader who is open about themselves and their positive and negative qualities immediately builds trust between themselves and their reports. By opening themselves up, they encourage others to reciprocate. Think about the opposite approach, where senior executives float in and out of the office building like ghosts. They tell you as little as possible about anything but the essential information regarding the job in hand. Would you trust them? Would you go that extra mile to ensure their objectives are achieved? Probably not. There is absolutely nothing to hang that trust on, except that perhaps they have always delivered at work.

This may be a case of imposter syndrome, where some leaders over-compensate when they feel they are not up to the job. This can also manifest itself among the senior team, sending everything out of balance because no one is being their authentic self. If you feel that there is a little of this in your organisation, or are maybe suffering from it yourself, there is another really useful exercise you can do here, which is basically an extension of the approaches used by Charles Stickland and Gregory Smith. Get your team together around a large table in as relaxed an environment as possible. Ask everyone in the room to imagine themselves 30 years in the future and to share what they would say to their present selves. What words of wisdom did they think they'd be given? I did this exercise with a team once and the results were fascinating. So many people there that day said almost the same thing in the guise of their future selves:

'Don't worry about things so much.'

'People are not judging you as much as you think.'

'I didn't know what the hell I was doing, but that was fine.'

Once a few people began to open up, others were more willing to share. There were some really open responses around the table and a few tears were even shed. It was clear that around half the people in the room had experienced at least some degree of imposter syndrome. Until that time, those half-dozen executives had been feeling a little lost and wondering when they were going to be found out. The responses of those who didn't seem to be suffering from imposter syndrome were equally interesting. They looked gobsmacked when they heard about the vulnerabilities of their colleagues. They really had no idea.

'Don't be ridiculous – we really value you,' they responded.

'But you're the best sales director we've ever had!'

The whole thing was a very revealing and useful exercise. It really benefited everyone on the team, both 'imposters' and non-imposters. I think it helped them all to be more authentic in their future dealings with one another and far more flexible in their responses to various challenges.

OPENNESS AND HONESTY

Working at building a relationship of trust requires a leader to be consistently open and honest with their team. Some leaders find this a very difficult skill to master, whereas some naturally trust others from the outset. If you are not sure where you sit on this scale, think about it via a bucket analogy. For those who are inclined to trust someone at the first meeting, their trust bucket always starts off full. Their faith in human nature is such that they will trust someone until they show them that they've made a big mistake. Occasionally, two individuals may disappoint each other a little and the trust bucket will empty a bit, but it is quite rare for individuals to make such a big mistake that the trust bucket is completely drained.

At the other end of the scale are individuals whose trust bucket is invariably empty on a first meeting. They are firmly in the trust-needs-to-be-earned camp. This is not to say that they find the other party untrustworthy; it is just that they have not yet seen anything to give them any evidence to fill the bucket. Over time, when this evidence is shown, the bucket will slowly fill up towards a time when there is complete trust and a solid relationship has been forged.

We all have a predisposition towards one or the other extreme when it comes to easily trusting others or not. As with everything to do relating to balance, the best starting point is to understand where you naturally sit. If you are the person who trusts no one until they prove themselves, people might find you a little cold on first meeting. This is not always a great way to inspire people to follow you, so you may need to find a way to compensate by seeking ways to quickly build a rapport. The getting-to-know-you chats detailed above can be particularly helpful in this case. Alternatively, if you tend towards being too trusting, you may open yourself up to the odd disappointment. Overall, the balanced approach is to use some evidence to support your decisions. In the absence of evidence, though, my instinct is to trust first until the situation proves you should do otherwise. While it is easier to not trust people, if you do this they will never feel close enough to you to prioritise your needs. In every case, though, always be clear about where the line is and what you won't tolerate.

What you will need to consider is how far you open up to build these essential relationships. Some leaders do find it difficult to maintain the right balance between personal and professional boundaries when it comes to working with their team. By necessity, leaders spend many hours with the people they work with, and to have an effective two-way relationship it is necessary to share a little about their personal lives. There are many leaders who find sharing personal details an almost impossible challenge.

I once worked with a chief executive who was enormously reluctant to blur the line between work and personal life. In fact, he rarely mentioned any personal stuff at all. While it is understandable to want to keep one's home life separate from work, it is very difficult for those around you to really trust you if you are not willing to open up a bit. Sharing experiences is how good relationships develop.

I managed to persuade this particular boss to run an off-site event at his home. It was amazing because everyone on the team saw a different side to him completely. The result was that the quality of the conversation we had around the garden table was brilliant. The chief executive relaxed and everyone else relaxed too. The conversation flowed and, for the first time ever, everyone felt emboldened to raise the real issues.

Of course, achieving this sort of work/life balance is not always straightforward. When leaders become close friends with a handful of direct reports, the lines do get blurry. This is particularly so if friendship is not extended to the rest of the team. When this happens, accusations of favouritism begin to fester. Similarly, while it is good to allow employees to see your human side, you also need to know when to draw the line. Sure, leaders should make an appearance at a work social event, but they should never be the last one standing, propping up the bar at the end of the night.

Opening up with the team is not the same thing as ceding control. It is important to encourage honesty and trust among the whole team. Similarly, the team members and the leader should challenge each other, but there is a time and place for it. And it's not in public. American politician and retired four-star general Colin Powell is widely credited with summing this up neatly. Reputedly, his view was that when he was in a room with his team, he always expected their unbridled, unfiltered views, whether or not the people on the team thought that he'd like them.

That is what loyalty meant to him. However, when they all left that room after a robust discussion and started to sell the plan he'd settled upon, he expected the team to deliver it as though they'd come up with it themselves. For this to work, the bond of trust and the quality of the relationships must be strong, and that doesn't just happen by accident.

There is also a point to be made here about not letting one person's opinion dominate – or standing back and allowing a team member to constantly be negative about the plan or other members of the team. This will bring down the atmosphere of collaboration and affect everyone. Ultimately, it will have an impact on performance too. If this is the case, serious consideration needs to be given to moving this individual on, even if they are one of the most talented people in the organisation. No one individual is more important than all the rest, and failure to act signals to everyone that they are perceived to be so. If this imbalance appears to be happening, act quickly. It is a clear sign of loss of control.

REAP THE BENEFITS OF DIVERSITY OF THOUGHT

Something else we need to be aware of here is diversity. We are inclined to more readily trust people who look like us or who have a similar background. I am instinctively drawn to trust those who have been in the armed services, even though I know that soldiers and sailors can let you down now and again. If you are aware of the fact that you tend to generalise too readily, pause for a moment, ask some getting-to-know-you questions and rethink. There is also a big argument here for looking more closely at the make-up of your team. If you always gravitate towards people who are similar, are you giving yourself the best chance for success?

Most people are familiar with the TV game show *Who Wants to Be a Millionaire*, which has been on our screens since 1998. Contestants, who are offered large cash prizes for correctly answering a series of multiple-choice questions, are in certain circumstances allowed to call upon the help of a friend, an expert or a poll of the audience. It's a fair bet to expect that the expert would be the most proficient in offering the right answer, and statistics show specialists are right more than half of the time. But the most effective source is the audience, which is successful more than nine times out of ten.

Why is this? Well, the size of the group helps, since a larger statistical sample will inevitably produce a more accurate average. Yet, it is the *diversity* of the group that is most crucial. Put simply, a diverse group has a better chance of weighing up the options and delivering a balanced, and therefore more accurate and effective, decision.

A far more serious and indeed tragic example of this principle in action concerns the complete failure of the Central Intelligence Agency (CIA) to prevent the 9/11 terrorist attacks. For decades the agency prided itself on its strident recruitment process, yet it spectacularly ignored the fact that nearly every new joiner was white and male, and from an Anglo-Saxon and Protestant background. Inevitably, these teams validated the beliefs of their colleagues, leading to some huge blind spots when it came to the threat posed by Osama bin Laden. They simply could not believe that the 'tall Saudi with a beard, squatting around a campfire, could be a threat to the United States of America'.[18] History, tragically, proved them very wrong.

There is so much more to diversity than simply ticking a box to show an organisation is inclusive and employs a good mix in terms of both race and gender. A diverse workforce is crucial to the success of a firm because it facilitates a truly balanced viewpoint. Well-balanced firms benefit from exploring different perspectives, and from having a collective intelligence that is greater than the sum of the parts. They reap the benefits of these differences in thinking.

For those who are not convinced, there is a wealth of information that backs up the advantages of diversity. Take the role of women in business. A 2011 survey by non-profit organisation Catalyst found a 26% difference in return on invested capital (ROIC) between the top-quartile companies, with boards made up of 19–44% women, and bottom-quartile companies, which had no women directors.[19]

TRUST BUT VERIFY

Trust between a leader and their reports is not the same as the leader completely absolving themselves of all accountability and involvement. It is perfectly acceptable, indeed encouraged, to check that what you asked to be done has indeed

---

18 Matthew Syed, 'Viewpoint: Was CIA 'too white' to spot 9/11 clues?' (BBC News, 9 September 2019), https://www.bbc.co.uk/news/world-us-canada-49582852.

19 Ray Williams, 'Why women may be better leaders for our times' (Ray Williams, 5 June 2019), https://raybwilliams.medium.com/why-women-may-be-better-leaders-for-our-times-85df7d47f825.

been done. It is very unwise to simply assume this is the case or try to keep the peace by not questioning things too closely. Trust is crucial but everyone still needs to do their job. There is a very useful process that applies here, which is known as 'trust but verify'. The concept first gained international recognition in 1986, during nuclear disarmament talks between US President Ronald Reagan and the Soviet leader, Mikhail Gorbachev. 'Trust but verify' is actually a Russian proverb, which Reagan was encouraged to use to help cement the relationship with his Soviet counterpart. The phrase went on to be used as a shorthand to describe the extensive verification process, where the US and the Soviet Union proved that they had fully complied with the hard-won disarmament treaty. Satellite images played a key role in the US proving that they had decommissioned certain nuclear capabilities. First they parked a large number of their bombers, that had been capable of delivering nuclear payloads, in the desert in Nevada. The bombers' wings were removed and laid in the sand beside the aircraft. That way a Soviet satellite could fly over and take pictures that would prove the devices were defunct and unserviceable. After this event, 'trust but verify' became part of the public lexicon.

Today, 'trust but verify' has become a very well-known process in certain organisations, particularly safety-critical ones. Airlines trust that their ground teams do their jobs in getting their fleet ready to fly each day, but they don't simply assume that everything has been done satisfactorily. Thus, once the tasks are complete, there are a number of standard checks that are done to make sure everything is entirely safe and ready. In the military, there is a process called 'musters' to ensure that every single piece of equipment and weaponry is properly logged. Individuals are routinely asked to compare the quantities of physical equipment with carefully compiled lists, often re-counting equipment that has been counted many times before. Everyone accepts, unquestioningly, that this needs to be done. After all, the potential implications of losing a rifle, or even a single piece of ammunition, are pretty serious. No one wants to be in a situation where something is unaccounted for but no one can quite remember if and when anyone last checked. How do you track something down when the available information is that vague?

While 'trust but verify' has an accepted role in safety-critical organisations, there are clear advantages to making it a habit even in non-safety-critical organisations. If it is a regular occurrence, nothing will ever be forgotten or slip down the list of priorities unnoticed. It is also a clear signal of how important it is that everyone meets the required standards. If the team is 100% clear on what is required and it knows that there will be scrutiny, there is no temptation to take any shortcuts.

Ah, you might say, but who wants to work in an organisation where the boss is constantly checking up on everyone? Part of the reticence is most likely down to the word 'trust', which is incredibly emotive. Saying there's a need to verify is akin to saying that you don't trust the person concerned. What needs to be made clear is that this is not the case at all. Yes, there is complete trust in the team, but it makes business sense to verify processes on a regular basis. You need to detach the emotion from the word 'trust'. If 'trust but verify' is part of an accepted ongoing process, it becomes part of the culture. You could also turn this thought on its head. Most people don't like working in a vacuum. There'll be a little voice in their head saying, *well, if the boss never checks it, what's the point in making an effort?* This way, they will see that their actions do make a difference and are important in the progress towards achieving the organisation's goals.

The verification process also builds trust. To return to the example of the military muster, if the numbers are always bang on in every recount, it strengthens the bond of trust between the commander and, say, the sergeant who runs the ammo store. When something comes along requiring a person the commander can really put their full faith behind, it is quite likely that their first thoughts will turn to people like this sergeant. They've proved themselves time and time again, and now is the time to give them the opportunity to stretch their skills further.

When weighing up whom to trust and how much, a leader will often have to trust their intuition, or gut feeling as it is known, as much as the data in front of them. If at any point you sense that something is not right, or your bullshit detector is sounding the alarm, you are advised to listen to it. There are few people who don't realise, instinctively, that they are not getting the full picture. If the response to a question about whether or not something has been done is hesitant, the chances are that it hasn't. But this isn't necessarily the time to leap on the other party and start shouting. The correct approach is to ask for whatever it is that was initially requested to be completed by the end of the day. This gives the team member a chance to put things right (most probably by working through lunch!). You are not trying to catch them out and you don't want your actions to be thought of in that way. The important thing is to challenge any response you don't feel 100% satisfied about.

There is an element of emotional intelligence involved in spotting the especially clever bullshitters. The best advice here is to get into the habit of regular self-reflection. Take the time to look back on the events of each week and if the responses you have heard don't match up to the reality of what you have subsequently found, make a mental note of it. Once you have done this over a period of time, you will begin to build up a clearer picture about particular team members who are, perhaps, not quite as effective as they claim to be, or who don't have a particularly close relationship with the truth. Next time they say something has been done, you may need to question the results more closely.

Ultimately, if you can't build strong relationships with your team and trust them to work with and alongside you, then all of the balanced leadership spectrums are useless. If you want to take everyone with you, there needs to be an environment of psychological safety. They need to know that the person in charge is going to deliver and that everyone on the team has a key role in achieving this aim. Likewise, if team members make mistakes along the way, which they most likely will, they will feel safe in doing so, because they will know that they are not going to get shot down in flames. This will only work if a strong relationship is built and maintained.

CHAPTER TEN
DELEGATION AND ACCOUNTABILITY

During the peak of the first coronavirus lockdown, I had some interesting online conversations with many of the teams I coach. One question that I made a point of asking was: how is this different? How is this affecting the way we now work in terms of leadership? Every single leader I worked with was now managing remote teams, mostly with just a few days' or weeks' notice that this was going to happen. I was curious about the changes that had to be made to the way they managed their teams and how they now delegated individual tasks. Hardly surprisingly, the feedback I received was that things had changed substantially in terms of how the various teams operated. However, the leaders I spoke with admitted that things were still getting done as they wanted, even though their reports were no longer in the same building with their bosses breathing down their necks. Although organisations the length and breadth of the land now had little choice but to delegate and then trust individuals would get on with their tasks, people were more than stepping up to the plate.

One of the most enduring takeaways from these conversations came from one boss, who told me that the abiding emotions that he had experienced from the period were 'trust and pride'.

He said, 'It's easy to micromanage people when we're all

close together, but at the moment, we're not, so we need to trust people. I have to trust that they will get on with it and that they really care enough about what we deliver to the client. And then, when they do deliver on it and they come good on something, I just feel this most immense sense of pride.'

His was not the only emotional reaction to the success of teams in their new isolated environments. While many of the leaders I spoke with had initially been unsure, each one had been impressed at how their teams came through. It had been a fantastic result in difficult circumstances.

It's too early to tell what the long-term impacts of the coronavirus will be. However, it is reasonable to assume that many people will have different expectations around how and where they work.

People are, quite rightly, questioning the point of having all those desks in London, New York, Singapore or any other big city. Why do businesses need to get everyone in at 9am and shove them all out again at 5pm? After stepping back and spending time away from it all, it seems nuts that everyone on the team has to get expensive peak trains into the city, all at the same time, and then leave together to travel home on crowded trains. Yet, until the coronavirus, very few organisations looked at this way of doing things and concluded: *hang on, this is ridiculous – is there a better way of doing things?*

We have now been shown, in a very vivid way that, yes, there is a better and more efficient way of running many organisations and delegating tasks remotely. Not everyone needs to sit in an office from 9am to 5pm to do their job effectively. A big enabler of this success is, of course, the internet. We wouldn't have been able to make any of these changes without it. Not only has the World Wide Web kept us all in constant touch via Zoom, Skype or FaceTime, but it is also an essential part of managing workflows. There is now a range of dashboards and tools where remote teams can track progress, divide up tasks and generally keep the show on the road.

The shift to a more independent, remote style of working means that many bosses will need to rethink the way they delegate. In the pre-lockdown days, I worked with many leadership teams that were very reluctant to let go. Declaring that they 'loved to solve problems', they'd always be the first to jump in and get stuck in on any and all of the urgent situations that threatened teams and departments. Then, they'd wonder why their firm was sliding into debt or veering off course. I used to have to explain to them that things were off-kilter because they were not doing their job. They were trying to do everyone else's job and were too easily distracted by busily firefighting today's problems.

This type of behaviour has a number of detrimental effects that throw a business off balance. Firstly, it is terrible for the development of the rest of the team. It creates complete co-dependence. If anything goes wrong, everyone knows to go and tell the boss. Workers fall into the routine of continuously identifying problems and passing them up the chain, but they never solve them. More importantly, while a leader is fixated on solving an urgent problem, how much time do they have to stop and think about potential new opportunities tomorrow? Even if new avenues are identified, they will never be properly pursued because everyone, including the leadership, is too focused on the here and now. This is not even to mention the crippling imbalance of running an organisation in a constant state of high adrenaline because everyone is anticipating the next blaze.

At the other end of the scale are leaders who do delegate; however, they always delegate to the same people. A clear sign that this has been happening is when 80% of the work is done by 20% of the organisation. Here, a leader has a short-list of go-to people: the top performers that they always bring in because they trust them to get the job done. The thinking seems to go that they've built this relationship over time and the top performers have never let them down, so they are a safe pair of hands. These trusted performers have such a shiny halo effect around them that when a new task is described in a meeting, they are the first person the leader thinks of to make it happen.

'Ah yes, let's give that to Claire,' is the automatic reaction.

Before you know it, Claire has everything on her plate. While yes, Claire is most likely super-efficient and supremely motivated, which is why she's always in the frame, this is a bit unfair. It puts undue pressure on Claire, who will always be drowning in work because she is so good. At the same time, it completely wastes the resources in the rest of the organisation.

STRETCH AND DEVELOP **EVERYONE**
The first rule of delegation must surely be to resist the temptation to always delegate to the person with the shiny halo and, instead, consider those others who need to be stretched

and developed further. If we return to the trusty bucket analogy, imagine that any organisation has four buckets of people (*see* Figure 12). There is the bucketful of Claires, who always get the job done brilliantly. Then there is also a bucketful of individuals who would probably do just as well if they were given the chance because they too are solid and trustworthy. These people are often overlooked in the rush to get the Claires involved. Next, there is a bucketful of people about whom leadership might be unsure but who, if they were stretched and developed a bit further, might well step up to the plate and surprise everyone. Finally, there is a bucketful of people who will require a great deal of hand-holding, but with time and a lot of encouragement will possibly flourish. (If your organisation has

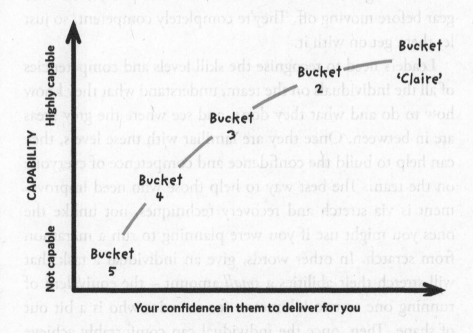

Figure 12. The confidence–capability dilemma

a fifth bucket filled with people who you feel are too useless to be asked to do anything meaningful, the question needs to be asked: why are they still working for you?) The point here is that you will never develop the people in buckets two and three, and indeed even four, if you keep going back to the Claires of this world.

Knowing your team well and understanding exactly where individuals are in the matrix is very important and this is not just so you can help to develop them so they reach the next stage. It also means you won't waste time encouraging or coaching people who really don't need this sort of input. Doing this is the equivalent of someone coming along and telling another person with 20 years of driving experience under their belt to start the engine, check all their mirrors and put the car into gear before moving off. They're completely competent, so just let them get on with it.

Leaders need to recognise the skill levels and competencies of all the individuals on the team, understand what they know how to do and what they don't, and see where the grey areas are in between. Once they are familiar with these levels, they can help to build the confidence and competence of everyone on the team. The best way to help those who need improvement is via stretch and recovery techniques, not unlike the ones you might use if you were planning to run a marathon from scratch. In other words, give an individual a task that will stretch their abilities a *small* amount – the equivalent of running one or two kilometres for a novice who is a bit out of shape. Then, once the individual can comfortably achieve that goal, introduce a new, slightly more ambitious one – say, a more taxing task that they may not have tried before. Perhaps one that's the equivalent of a five-kilometre jog, building on their successful two-kilometre run. This is the way to help individuals move on to the next stage in the matrix and to take some of the pressure off poor Claire.

Roderic and I often use the phrase 'delegate to the point of discomfort'. This is where a leader is really unsure whether or not it is in an individual's capabilities to undertake a task, or whether the leader would be better off shouldering it themselves. As a rule, I would say, *if in doubt, give it to them*. More often than not, they will surprise you.

ANALYSE THE STATUS OF THE TASK

Stretch goals are much easier to set if you are very clear about the status of the task they relate to. When Roderic and I first started to discuss this and how we might best explain it to our coaching groups, our joint thought process brought us to the task-delegation system that is routinely used on large naval vessels. Things break down all the time on ships, both large and small. It's just what happens. However, there is a world of difference between, say, a lightbulb blowing in the galley and a catastrophic fault in the system that converts salt water into fresh. Both problems need to be logged by the ship's personnel, who will then delegate the tasks required to fix them according to the problems' urgency. Clearly, in this instance, an imminent lack of fresh water is much more pressing than a slightly more dim visual atmosphere in the galley. Thus, a numerical system is used where, if an issue is logged as a category four problem, it means the ship has to immediately return to port for urgent repairs. Category one, at the other end of the scale, means that the task needs to be addressed but it can wait. It is not mission critical. Category two and three faults fall somewhere in between essential and non-mission-critical. The categories help the commanders and everyone else on the vessel to make decisions about what to prioritise. It's a great way to communicate too. If someone notes a category four problem, everyone jumps to it.

Roderic and I adapted this process for our Prioritisation Matrix, where the variables that need to be weighed up are: the value of the task to the individual using the matrix and their organisation's overall strategy, and whether the task falls into the bracket of the day-to-day running of the organisation (tactical activity) or is integral to its strategic future (strategic activity). Figure 13 shows the various pulls at play here.

The challenge for leaders at any level is to balance themselves on this graph. Organisations want their leaders to move towards the top right, where they bring their experience, knowledge and judgement. New leaders often want to stay at the bottom left, where they feel comfortable, because that is where they have lived up to now. And, in fact, it is often not just new leaders who prefer the safety and security of the bottom left – many senior leaders maintain that they have become senior because they're great at the tactical stuff. Therefore, what are supposed to be strategic, top-level conversations go straight into the weeds, and no one calls it out because they're all loving not having the stress of having to deal with these conversations! Activity in the 'grey area' requires particularly careful

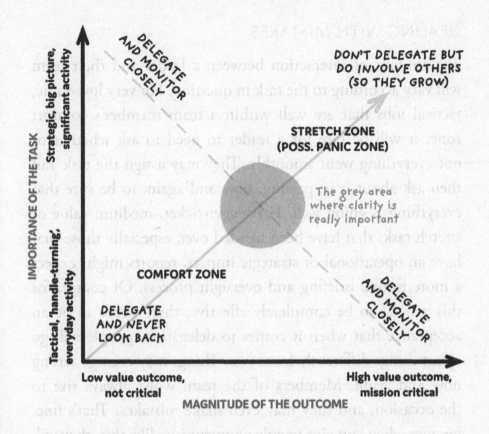

Figure 13. Leaders need to balance where they spend their time

management as it could fall foul of assumption and either be done twice or not at all.

I once coached someone who had taken on a significant new role and was struggling to get his head around what he needed to do. How much should he hold on to of his old role and what did he need to get rid of? I encouraged him to use the graph to plot his activities and, if they fell into the bottom left, to delegate. If they fell in the top right, these were things he needed to do himself, or at least retain significant control of them.

DEALING WITH MISTAKES

The amount of interaction between a leader and their team will vary according to the task in question. For very low-value, tactical jobs that are well within a team member's comfort zone, it will be rare for a leader to need to ask whether or not everything went smoothly. They may assign the task and then ask about it in passing, now and again, to be sure that everything is going well. For bigger-ticket, medium-value or stretch tasks that have been handed over, especially those that have an operational or strategic impact, reports might expect a more formal briefing and oversight process. Of course, for this process to be completely effective, there needs to be an acceptance that when it comes to delegation, people will go about things differently from you. Things may even go wrong now and again. Members of the team won't always rise to the occasion, and they may even make mistakes. That's fine, because when you give people opportunities like this, they will learn from them and most likely achieve the goal on the second or third attempt. It is all part of moving them on in the Situational Leadership Model. Be careful how you deal with mistakes, though. If you see something going badly and your instinct is to immediately hoist back control because you know you could do it better, pause and take a breath. The team will never develop if you do this and you will never have the freedom to do other, more strategic things. (And poor old Claire will be more overworked than ever!) Reacting like this is to the detriment of the whole organisation. It undermines everything you want to do in empowering the team.

There are variables. If, for example, there is an entirely new team, leadership may err on the side of control, shifting the emphasis in the Prioritisation Matrix. After all, at such times, a leader needs to keep a closer eye on events to understand what the team is working on and prioritising, and they will also be less willing to let mistakes happen until they know the team better. Then, once the team is fully engaged and everyone is comfortable with working together and with the tasks ahead, then the spectrum can be moved towards more flexibility and less control from leadership.

For all of this to work smoothly, a leader needs to give the team all the equipment, tools and support required for them to complete the tasks as assigned. In this respect, I am always reminded of the motto of the Royal Military Academy Sandhurst, where I received my training: 'Serve to Lead'. It is a paradox, but this seeming contradiction is at the heart of what makes a good leader in any circumstance, whether it is in the military or outside in civilian life. We are there to provide our team with all they need to do the job for us. In military scenarios, this might be weapons, body armour or food to keep everyone's energy up. We also need to make sure we provide them with moral support and provide a team and social structure so that they have a reason to care. Once we have provided all of these things, we can turn around and say: *this is what we have given you – now go and do your best work.* If you focus on the needs of the team, shaping them and helping them to deliver, their performance will improve. If you don't, and simply concentrate on your own wants and needs, don't be surprised if the team does not achieve what is asked of it.

One further useful skill that I would like to share – which is, I believe, crucial to successful delegation and keeping any misunderstandings and mistakes down to a minimum – is a technique called the 'back brief'. Here, a leader starts by bringing in everyone involved in a project and giving them a detailed brief on the task ahead. They outline the objectives, available budget and timelines, and they highlight potential issues they've identified that may need to be resolved. Once this is completed, they ask the person who will be leading the team assigned to the task to come back to them in a day, or perhaps two, to give them a back brief. During the back brief, the team leader repeats back their understanding of what they've heard. It is a great opportunity to be sure they have completely understood what they've been asked to do and are on the same page as the person who asked them to do it.

Why leave it a day or so, rather than asking for a back brief there and then on the first meeting? Well, it is useful to give anyone time to mull over the task ahead and reflect on it. It also gives them space to formulate questions as they weigh up how to achieve the task. These issues may only arise after everyone on the team has left the meeting, so it is helpful to give the project time to bed down in their minds.

Of course, if your teams are frequently coming back to you with wildly different interpretations in their back briefs, this is a sign that maybe you are not being as clear as you'd like to be. You should perhaps rethink and possibly even map out a new approach, before trying again. If you give them the same brief again, don't be surprised if nothing changes in your next brief back. Step back and rethink.

As more crucial projects move forward, meetings will need to be convened on a fairly regular basis to run through the state of play, examine progress towards deadlines and raise any potential challenges. The frequency of these meetings, whether it is weekly, fortnightly or monthly, will depend on the scale of the task and its importance to the organisation. These discussions are not about leaders taking control of tasks. They are predominantly about listening and together developing ways forward.

Bear in mind that the Prioritisation Matrix is never static. Circumstances change in any business. Something that looked like a distant, almost improbable threat may turn out to be a little more serious than first thought. Likewise, a significant project may turn out to not be that significant after all. Everyone will understand that, though. Business is fluid. However, with this sort of clarity, both on the task and on the people achieving it, it is easy for a leader to change emphasis and dial up or dial down the control, without confusing or frustrating the people around them. In turn, the people on the team will be inspired by the knowledge that when circumstances dictate, tasks will be properly delegated. Everyone will be given a chance to shine and the freedom to use their initiative.

Leaders will need to make decisions every day about how much of a task they themselves need to control, and how much can be handed over to the team. In the majority of cases, it is in everyone's interest that they delegate as much as possible. Even if a task is quite complex and feels like quite a stretch, the right course of action is to find a mechanism to allow themselves and everyone else to remain in balance.

A more crucial project, more forward, meetings will need to be convened on a fairly regular basis to run through the state of play, examine progress towards deadlines and raise any potential challenges. The frequency of these meetings, whether it is weekly, fortnightly or monthly, will depend on the scale of the task and its importance to the organisation. These discussions are not about leaders taking control of tasks. They are predominantly about listening and together developing ways forward.

Bear in mind that the Prioritisation Matrix is never static. Circumstances change in any business. Something that looked like a distant, almost improbable threat may turn out to be a little more serious than first thought. Likewise, a significant project may turn out not to be that significant after all. Everyone will understand that, though. Business is fluid. However, with this sort of clarity, both on the task and on the people achieving it, it is easy for a leader to change emphasis and dial up or dial down the control, without equating or frustrating the people around them. In turn, the people on the team will be inspired by the knowledge that, when circumstances dictate, tasks will be properly delegated. Everyone will be given a chance to shine and the freedom to use their initiative.

Leaders will need to make decisions every day about how much of a task they themselves need to control, and how much can be handed over to the team. In the majority of cases, it is in everyone's interest that they delegate as much as possible. Even if a task is quite complex and feels like quite a stretch, the right course of action is to find a mechanism to allow themselves and everyone else to remain in balance.

CHAPTER ELEVEN
FOCUS AND CLARITY

If you've ever seen a tightrope walker achieve their craft, you'll know what a marvel this feat can be. The artist has utter focus on their gravity-defeating task and is seemingly oblivious to everything around them as they make their way across the impossibly thin stretch of wire that takes them to their goal. Somehow, they manage to ignore all the distractions around them; whether it is the sighs of the admiring audience, perhaps a niggling worry they have at home, or the knowledge that they are going to have to repeat this performance all over again for the next paying crowd. They are entirely focused on the next step.

How do they achieve this, well, perfect balance? They manage it because they are 100% clear about what it is they want to achieve – getting to the other side – to the exclusion of all other distractions. This is a strategy that translates brilliantly to all aspects of life, whether it is personal goals, a vision for business growth or political ambitions. Perhaps one of the most famous manifestations of just how powerful a single, overarching goal can be when it comes to complete focus is President John F. Kennedy's May 1961 declaration, before a special joint session of Congress, that he wanted to send an American to the moon before the end of the decade. He created a really clear picture of the dramatic and ambitious goal he'd created.

After that, if you'd have asked anyone in the administration or NASA what they were trying to achieve, everyone would have spoken with one voice: we are all trying to put a man on the moon by the end of the decade. Everyone was completely aligned and working towards that single purpose. That is powerful.[20]

Leaders are always asking their teams to do more stuff. Try this, achieve that, make sure that this is completed by such-and-such a time. Yet, without the filter of how each task achieves the unified vision, it is really difficult for individual team members to understand the urgency or importance of each request. (It doesn't help that there is a tendency for leaders to keep giving their reports more and more things to do, with the assumption that they'll cram it all in. The reality is, they just can't.) Organisations prosper when everyone has a laser-like focus on achieving the overall strategy. Amazon are the perfect example of an organisation that adopted a laser-like focus. The company initially started selling books online. There were two reasons for this. The first is that they were able to store an online database of every book on earth without printing it out. The second is that books are relatively uniform and easy to post. They chose to sell a product that made it easy for them to get the logistics right. Amazon has become the enormous online marketplace it is today because they adopted a laser-like focus and didn't try to do too much.

A well-articulated goal also provides clarity about what does

20 John Nemo, 'What a NASA janitor can teach us about living a bigger life' (*Business Journals*, 23 December 23014), https://www.bizjournals.com/bizjournals/how-to/growth-strategies/2014/12/what-a-nasa-janitor-can-teach-us.html.

not need to be done. Most leaders spend the majority of their time creating new initiatives and asking their people to do more. Brilliant leaders are not afraid to ask them to do less – to stop doing things that don't contribute towards making the vision a reality. If everyone is focused on one clearly defined direction, people are less likely to head off in another, entirely unrelated one. This is especially useful for the people on the team who find it hard to say no or who may have a pet project that is not strictly contributing towards the main objective. Each task can be weighed against the goal and if it doesn't meet the criteria, it can be dispensed with.

Clarity about the big goal is not just vital to keeping the team on track: it plays a crucial role in keeping leadership focused too. We all face distractions each working day. There's the temptation to check your email to see whether that response has arrived and then, before you know it, you've stepped into a labyrinth of entirely different digital calls upon your time. Or, perhaps you step across the office to chat to a colleague about something very specific, but get stopped on the way to be asked about an entirely unrelated matter. According to one survey, the average employee is interrupted between 50 and 60 times per day, or once every eight minutes. And the more senior you are in an organisation, the more distractions you get. It takes up to two hours a day to recover from distractions and get things back on track. The worst part of it is, 80% of these interruptions are judged as unnecessary.[21]

---

21 Rudi Dalman, 'The real cost of interruptions at work' (*People*, 12 May 2016), https://www.peoplehr.com/blog/2016/05/12/the-real-cost-of-interruptions-at-work.

CREATE THINKING TIME

It's not easy to think about the big picture when the world keeps spinning relentlessly forward, with new challenges day after day and constant demands for instant results. But, for true progress to be made, leaders need to make time to visualise and work out how to pursue the big picture. A good way to do this is to follow in the footsteps of Microsoft founder Bill Gates, who has 'Think Weeks' several times a year. He physically takes himself off, out of the day-to-day bustle, and seeks out a place where he can find inspiration and go deep into a few areas of interest. He uses the opportunity to focus in on a number of essays and briefs written and submitted by his team on a range of subject headings. To show you how effective this can be, did you know that one of his Think Weeks in the nineties was dedicated to the subject of the 'Internet Tidal Wave'? I'm sure you will agree that his subsequent actions show the value of this deep-dive thinking process. The Think Week strategy is now emulated by several Silicon Valley bosses who are clearly hoping for some of the Microsoft magic.[22]

It is an incredibly useful, enriching and refreshing experience to take yourself off and dive deeply into the future of an organisation. Clearly, it is best done away from the office, otherwise it is all too easy to be dragged back into the day-to-day. As a general rule, it is useful to find somewhere that is conducive to learning and reflection. Plan your time carefully, and organise in advance background material around areas,

---

22 Julian Hayes II, 'In the 1980s, Bill Gates would escape to a secret cabin in the woods to protect himself from burnout. Here's the modern-day, easier version of his approach' (*Inc.*, 2 August 2019), https://www.businessinsider.com/bill-gates-took-think-weeks-the-1980s-launched-internet-explorer-2019-8?r=US&IR=T.

or themes, that seem of most interest, or that have been at the top of your mind for a while. That way, you can focus on what you are interested in, rather than taking a scattergun approach. There doesn't need to be one single subject area, but it is wise to limit the number of topics. It may also be helpful to set up a defined list of expected outcomes. Think Week fans advocate exercise as an important part of the process, whether it is a cycle through country lanes or a walk on the beach. It should go without saying that this is all about getting away from the distractions of daily life, so that also means limiting Wi-Fi and web-browsing. Keep phone calls to a minimum and avoid scheduling any meetings during your Think Week.

I suspect many leaders will be resistant to this idea, worrying about what will be going on back at base in their absence. The success or otherwise of a Think Week is predicated on the fact that an environment has been created where the organisation being left behind is operating smoothly. If the leader's usual role is consumed by putting out daily fires, this might not be so easy (although, arguably, a step back here is more pertinent than ever since it suggests a leader has got far too close to the other end of the spectrum and is so far into the detail that they can't extract themselves). The way around this is to work towards documenting standards and processes ahead of a Think Week, so managers understand them and their role in delivering them; that way, there is more of an opportunity to step back, albeit briefly. Leaders may also assume that they need to be seen all the time, in order to motivate the troops. This chimes with the traditional, yet ultimately misguided, view that working means sitting in the office behind a laptop, reading, writing and sending emails: that is how things get done. My riposte to this would always be: unless your customers pay you to read, write and send emails, then that is not working. It is just something you need to do to achieve your goal. Indeed, the further you go up an organisational hierarchy, the more you need to take a step back and think about the long-term implications for the organisation.

EVERYONE MUST BE COMMITTED TO THE GOAL

Throughout this book, there have been numerous examples of teams that were entirely committed to one goal. What President Kennedy, the British rowing team, Team Sky and Henderson Global Investors have all shown us is that when an organisation decides upon, and then focuses everyone's attention on, one overarching goal, amazing things happen. It becomes the metric that all other things are measured against, and all other distractions are ignored. Of course, it is crucial that the message is powerful and succinct: we are going to the moon, or we are going to win the Tour de France! If you get this part wrong and make the message too long or convoluted, or attempt to shoehorn in two or three points while pretending they are one, the overwhelming reaction will be one of confusion and, quite possibly, bemusement. Hardly surprisingly, no one on the team will know exactly why they are there or what they stand for. They'll understand their individual roles, but not what they are supposed to be working towards as a team.

For a team to get behind a goal, things need to be kept

simple. In the book *The One Thing: The Surprisingly Simple Truth Behind Extraordinary Results*, the authors Gary Keller and Jay Papasan argue that we should all choose one thing that we want to achieve each day.[23] This doesn't mean that we completely fail to do anything else, but rather that this one thing is our number one focus. Having a succinct, easy-to-get-behind goal that everyone completely understands makes this process much, much easier.

Once that one clear goal has been agreed upon, everyone needs to be told about it. And this is where clarity comes in. In one of my first jobs after leaving the army, I remember sitting around a table with my colleagues while the person running the business explained his vision. He was a bright guy with a first-class degree in microbiology from Cambridge, but I honestly couldn't decipher a word of what he was telling us. It just felt like he was spouting a series of words and they didn't particularly seem to fit together all that well either. A glance around the room at the blank faces of my colleagues revealed that I was not alone in this view. This boss was clear in his mind about what he wanted to do. The thinking behind it was absolutely crystal clear to him. Unfortunately, the message wasn't getting through. Eventually, we encouraged the boss to draw us a picture. I am being perfectly serious here. Drawing a picture of goals may not always appear to be reasonable or practical, but it is certainly a thought process worth considering. We all have different learning and listening styles: some people like reading, others listening and others seeing pictures.

23 Gary Keller with Jay Papasan, *The One Thing: The Surprisingly Simple Truth Behind Extraordinary Results* (London: John Murray, 2014).

To get a message across in a clear and impactful way, it can be helpful to communicate it in as many ways as possible.

The job is not over after the goal has been explained to the team once. All too often, organisations come up with these goals and announce them with a great fanfare at a big town hall event – and then they are never mentioned again. You may even have experienced such a launch yourself. For some reason, the people behind the announcement never seem to notice that 20% of the organisation are not present at the event, a further 40% who were there were probably not listening properly, and the rest will have forgotten what was said by the time they get back to their desks. Of those who did hear the message, many might not have understood it at all.

To make sure everyone is committed to working towards a goal, it needs to be repeated over and over again. You may think that you've said it ten times and that will do, but it won't. You need to say it 40 or 50 times. At least. Keep saying it until you are sick to death of it. By this stage you can safely assume that everyone on the team has heard it at least twice. If, however, you ask ten people on the team what they believe to be the overall strategy of the organisation and receive wildly differing answers, this is a cause for deep concern. Either your single message was not clear in the first place, or you still haven't said it enough.

There is a big difference between setting a goal and then communicating it effectively so it sticks. We could all do well to take a leaf out of the book of the nuclear industry (which Roderic used to work in). Each meeting was started with a 'safety moment', which underlined the importance of the

100% safety goal in this industry. It has to be part of the culture and it is. As Roderic says, it sounds painful, but it really needn't be. It only takes a moment to ask a question, such as, 'When was the last time the first alarms were tested?' Doing so constantly underlines the importance of the goal and maintains everyone's focus on what is most important to the organisation.

SET BOUNDARIES

Once everyone is crystal clear about their own roles and what they are expected to achieve, a leader can define the boundaries around the tasks required. They can articulate how far individuals on the team are allowed to push things in the pursuit of that goal. Boundaries define how much time and effort people can spend on tasks. They give individuals on the team the room to be creative and bring their own expertise to bear. They know what they have to achieve and now can work out the optimal way to do so. This, in turn, will give them leeway to try and fail, which we all need to do in order to learn and progress. As we saw in the previous chapter, everyone needs to be given a degree of freedom. It is an important part of people's development.

Freedom to innovate, yet within boundaries, is also extremely powerful for building strong relationships with the team. It gives the leadership the flexibility to step back now and again, and not interject when they see people heading off on a course that might not be helpful. Yes, the individual may not succeed, but think about how much they will learn in the process.

Once the boundaries are known, there are other things that leaders can do to help individual members of the team to focus on working to their best abilities on a person-by-person basis. One useful way to get a lot more out of a team is to look closely at its members' preferred working styles.

There's a really useful blog post on this subject by Paul Graham (of Y Combinator fame), who identified two sorts of working styles: the managers and the makers.[24] You're probably most familiar with the manager's schedule. Here a day is broken down into chunks of an hour or so, with different activities in each segment. When a meeting is required, it is easily slotted into one of these slots without having an impact elsewhere. A maker's schedule is a little different. These are people like, say, coders or writers – people who make things or who do anything creative. They generally divide their day into two: morning and afternoon (and sometimes they don't divide the day up at all). They need time to think about what they are doing, prepare and then give their work the intensity of focus it requires. Slotting in a meeting mid-morning or mid-afternoon with people like this is a disaster. They won't have time to get anything meaningful done beforehand or afterwards. There is a cascading effect too, in that if they know they are going to have to interrupt their day, makers feel it's hardly worth getting started. They don't find it easy to simply switch from one mode to another.

If you are on a manager's schedule, it can be hard to conceptualise how much those on a maker's schedule can be thrown

24 Paul Graham, 'Maker's schedule, manager's schedule' (*Paul Graham*, July 2009), http://www.paulgraham.com/makersschedule.html.

off track by an ill-scheduled meeting, or even a casual 'let's grab a coffee and have a chat'. But, once you know this is an issue, it's great to work around it. Meetings can be scheduled at the end of the maker's day, or by encouraging them to set aside a chunk of time once a week for discussions. Give them the space to work in the best way for them and their focus levels will increase exponentially.

A similar concept is espoused by Cal Newport, an associate professor of computer science at Georgetown University, who has written extensively about how to use focus to achieve career success. In *Deep Work: Rules for Focused Success in a Distracted World*, he argues that there are two core skills required to succeed today: mastering deep thinking and being able to produce at an elite level.[25] This is something that is not easy thanks to the many distractions we all experience every day, from social media to email. The onus is on leadership to create an environment where each team member is given time and space to give their tasks their full, undivided attention. Newport suggests that people schedule time for unbroken concentration, making it a daily habit. This will generally be time that individuals feel at their most productive. In my case, it is at the end of the day, even during the evening (family commitments permitting), whereas Roderic says he does his best intensive work first thing in the morning and endeavours to make sure that meetings are never scheduled during these hours. At the other end of the scale, individuals are also encouraged to schedule slots for internet time and even allocate a 30-minute slot to switch

25 Cal Newport, Deep Work: Rules for Focused Success in a Distracted World (London: Piatkus, 2016).

off and be a bit lazy from time to time. This more measured approach results in increased focus and allows individuals to take a deep dive into their work and be most productive when they do. A change in culture to allow this style of working will always be led from the top. Leaders need to give their teams the room to set their schedules and encourage them to work in a way that helps them be most productive.

There is also a big opportunity here for a leader to speak with individuals on the team to find out *where* they believe they do their best work. If you think about it, many people find it extremely distracting to be in an office environment. We know this because these are the ones who always have their heads down and headphones in, doing their best to block out the sounds of the rest of the office. Every firm has individuals like this. Yes, these same people might enjoy the social side of the office and like creating connections with others, but they are also crying out for a quiet space to do some of that deep thinking. It is important to recognise who these people are and to create an environment where they can do their thinking without distractions.

Not everyone will want to isolate from their colleagues to do their best work either. Another thing that we discovered from the coronavirus lockdowns was that many people much prefer to be in the office. They find this space far more conducive to getting work done. The point is to have these conversations and to help everyone work in a way that allows them to be the most productive.

When applying focus and clarity, a final skill we recommend is to always, always make a note of what it is you have

asked people to do. Any leader who is in the habit of direct-
ing the team and then moving on will very soon find that the
team drifts off task. They know they won't be chased, so why
tear themselves apart trying to achieve what they've been asked
to do? The implied underlying message when things are not
followed up on is that the task was not really that important
in the first place. Keeping in touch with progress is how you
create accountability. Figure 14 illustrates this idea.

ACTION	OWNER	DISCUSSED	EMAILED	COMMITTED DATE	ACTION COMPLETE
Prepare for webinar	RY	N/A	N/A	25/11	Y
Complete VAT return	RS	N/A	Y	29/11	Y
Review accounts	RY	Y	Y	29/11	
Book accom for 2–4 Dec	MS	Y	N/A	28/11	
Prepare for MS speech	RY	N/A	N/A	12/12	
Learn how to record webinars	MS	Y	Y	4/12	

Figure 14. Use processes

CHAPTER TWELVE
ENGAGEMENT AND MOTIVATION

Roderic and I talk about principles all the time. To us, they are the basis of how to do things. They've become hardwired into our brains thanks to our military backgrounds. We therefore know that the first principle of war is the selection of the aim, which requires clarity and focus. The second principle is the maintenance of morale, which requires keeping people motivated and engaged in what they are doing. Thus, leadership needs to be clear on what it is going to do, and then keep this front and centre of mind; and this goal needs to be supported by keeping everyone's morale up.

Motivation and engagement are crucial components in any balanced organisation, not just in the armed services. If morale is bad or begins to dip, it is impossible to do anything meaningful. Employee engagement is the secret to longevity and consistent growth in any organisation. Share knowledge and information with employees, reward them for a job well done, and encourage them to become fully immersed with the operation and there is more chance an organisation will consistently prosper both in good times and in bad.

Whenever anyone speaks about employee engagement, the immediate example you think of is the adoption of the employee ownership or partnership model. Yet, while the partnership ideal is admirable (since every employee is fully invested in the business as a part owner) it can only ever be as good as the individuals involved. It doesn't prevent there being a toxic atmosphere in a particular store because one manager is not engaged, meaning their reports aren't either. For engagement to be effective, *everyone* needs to be involved on an emotional level. To be properly engaged and motivated, each member of the team needs to have their heart in it as well as their head. Emotional engagement is key. If you have emotional skin in the game, you are far, far more likely to work diligently, even passionately, towards the goal. Consider any significant military failure and you will see the truth in this.

MONEY ISN'T EVERYTHING

The mistake that many leaders make is to believe that they can throw money at the issue of engagement and motivation. Nothing motivates more than cold, hard cash, right? Actually, this is not true. There is a big assumption about motivation that says if you reward something, you get more of the behaviour you want, whereas if you punish something, you get less of the behaviour you don't want. However, this is actually not true at all in the majority of cases. Daniel Pink, the author of *Drive: The Surprising Truth about What Motivates Us*, has done some interesting research in this respect.[26] He found that, yes, when a task involves only mechanical skills, a blunt instrument like a straight monetary reward does encourage better performance. However, if even rudimentary cognitive skills are required, financial incentives can actually lead to poorer performance.

26 Daniel H. Pink, *Drive: The Surprising Truth about What Motivates Us* (New York: Riverhead Books, 2009).

Of course, if you don't pay people enough, they won't ever be motivated. The right starting point is to pay everyone the going rate so that the issue of money is not on the table. After that, Pink found that the three factors that most motivate people are autonomy, mastery and purpose. Autonomy is the desire to direct our own lives and have power over what we do and how we do it. Mastery is the urge we all have to get better at things, which is why people spend hours practising a musical instrument or learning a language. Finally, purpose is the desire to do something that has meaning, which is a powerful motivator because we all want to think that we make a difference. If you can provide your team with autonomy, an opportunity for mastery and a purpose, they will be infinitely more motivated and engaged than if you simply throw money at them.

This theory was tested to its limits during the first coronavirus lockdown in the UK, when all the usual rules changed and barely anyone was going into the workplace. There was no opportunity for bosses to breathe down their teams' necks and punish poor performance. Instead, there was a lot of reliance on people finding their own way in working out how to do their jobs in an unusual environment. This required all three of the motivational tools cited by Pink – autonomy, mastery and purpose – and it was, we believe, a great deal of the reason why the working-from-home 'experiment' proved so popular among so many (although by no means all, as explored towards the end of the previous chapter).

To see how powerful this independent working can be in the long term, we can look at a great example that had been running for many years prior to the pandemic. The example comes courtesy of Matt Mullenweg, the founder of Automattic, the company behind WordPress, the software tool that powers 35% of all websites on the internet. After founding Automattic in 2005, Matt decided very early on that he did not want a central office in San Francisco. He had big ambitions to grow the company and didn't see why he should fish from a relatively small pool of digital developers. The world is full of talented people – why not work with them? Thus, he built the company entirely with the services of remote developers. Today, Automattic, which boasts a valuation of $3 billion, has 1170 employees scattered across 75 countries, speaking 93 languages.[27] The company has been built around Daniel Pink's three principles of motivation and, as the numbers suggest, it seems to be going pretty well. Each member of the remote team makes their own decisions about the time they work and how they structure things. They are entirely self motivated.

Aside from the obvious improvements in productivity that come from encouraging autonomy, mastery and purpose, this is a better scenario for leadership too. Rather than spending (read: wasting) time on cracking the whip, it leaves time for those at the top to use their energy on productive thinking.

DEFINE PERSONAL GOALS

To properly engage people, you need to find what really affects them as individuals. What is it that gets them to work each

---

27 Steve Glaveski, 'The five levels of remote work – and why you're probably at Level 2' (SG, 30 March 2020), https://www.steveglaveski.com/blog/the-five-levels-of-remote-work-and-why-youre-probably-at-level-2.

day? What do they truly value? If you can find that out and find a way to tap into it and support it, your efforts will benefit both parties.

Look at any chief executive who heads up an organisation of any size and, in the vast majority of cases, they are there by design – their own design. They had a plan to get to the top in their chosen field and carefully worked out their route to success. They took one job and then another, in a series of stepping stones towards their ultimate goal. They probably have a similar intense focus in their ambitions for their family's future, laying out where they want to live, where their children will go to school and so on. This is what motivates and engages them, every single day.

Doesn't it make sense to mirror the process followed by chief executives, who carefully map out their own careers? It can be a brilliant tactic for the rest of the team. After all, what could possibly be more motivating and engaging than making sure everyone is focused on their own personal goals, as well as those of the organisation as a whole?

One of the key questions any leader should be asking their reports is: where do you want to be in five or ten years' time? Where do you feel your long-term career direction is taking you? Not everyone will have thought about it, certainly not in clear terms. If an individual doesn't know, that's fine. It is a leader's role to help them develop clarity on those questions. Alternatively, an individual may already have a clear idea and that is great. What is most important is that everyone is encouraged to articulate these goals. Once they do, the leadership can work towards aligning the ambitions of each individual with the goals of the organisation they work for, so the two things are mutually beneficial.

The clichéd answer to the question 'Where do you want to be in ten years' time?' is 'To be in the boss's chair', but there is absolutely nothing wrong if this is the response you get. If anyone on the team does articulate this, it's a great starting point. This is the time to fire up LinkedIn and to start exploring the career paths of other chief executives. How did they get to their position? The next step is to work with this ambitious individual to begin to plan how to get a broad selection of experience so they can start climbing the career ladder. While always being sure to stick closely to the corporate goal, the aim is to focus on their personal development in parallel. Do this and it will resonate with that individual and keep them focused and engaged. By aligning their goals with the goals of the organisation, they will see they have some potential for progression.

Roderic describes an instance where this worked very effectively indeed. He was working with a recruitment company that had been careful to get clarity on what all the members of its sales team wanted to achieve. By far the majority of the team had a similar goal. The firm, which was mainly staffed by people in their twenties and early thirties, saw a groundswell in ambition among team members who wanted to own their own homes. Nearly everyone declared that they were saving for a deposit with the aim of buying a property within the next five years. Armed with this information, the business changed the entire structure of the language used for its commission and incentives. Instead of calling the annual bonus a 'bonus', they renamed it the 'house deposit fund'. They recognised the ambitions of the team and aligned its targets towards what the individuals on the team wanted to do, which in turn boosted sales, which is what the recruitment firm wanted to achieve.

If the business's success will help someone achieve their own goals, they are unlikely to have any difficulty feeling engaged. Thus, leaders need to have that conversation first, to find out what incentives will work best.

While the individuals at the recruitment agency were all strongly motivated by the idea of getting a foot on the bottom rung of the housing ladder, it would be wrong to assume that everyone is always motivated by the same things as everyone else on the team. You won't know what each individual wants until you have that conversation, though.

The book *There Is an I in Team: What Elite Athletes and Coaches Really Know about High Performance*, by University of Cambridge professor Mark de Rond, challenges popular notions about teams.[28] After studying a number of sporting teams, including his university's renowned rowing squad, de Rond concluded that contrary to all the gung-ho rhetoric about teamwork, it is actually crucial to treat immensely talented performers as individuals. A dominant focus on the singular goal of achieving perfect harmony between all team members can actually be hugely damaging to overall performance.

While rowing squads need to act in faultless unison and the pace of the blades entering and leaving the water needs to be completely seamless, each member of the squad has very

---

28 Mark de Rond, *There Is an I in Team: What Elite Athletes and Coaches Really Know about High Performance* (Boston: Harvard Business School, 2012).

different motivations. Yes, they want their team to win (and the Cambridge team is only there for one reason – despite rowing in all sorts of tournaments, the only real goal is to beat Oxford!) but each member also wants to be recognised for their own performance. They have egos and want to be in a particular prime seat on the boat, or play a certain role. It is the same in any team. All teams are made up of a bunch of individuals with their own needs, motivations, desires and aspirations. While it is crucial that a good leader builds a sense of shared endeavour through inspiring, engaging and motivating a team, they also need to engage them as the individuals they are. The leader needs to find a way to help each person channel their formidable talents to the collective good while still letting them do what they do best. It's not an easy balance to achieve. There is a very helpful model here, known as Action-Centred

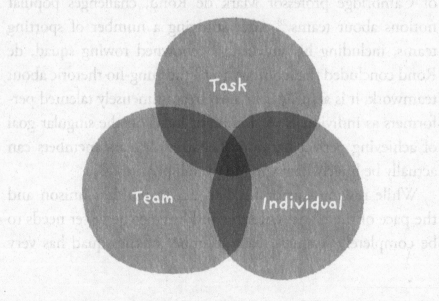

Figure 15. Action-centred leadership

Leadership, by academic and leadership expert John Adair[29] (*see* Figure 15).

Adair's model is based on three overlapping circles representing the following:

- Achieve the task
- Build and maintain the team
- Develop the individual

The circles need to overlap because no one person alone can accomplish the task. Also, if the needs of the team are not met, the task will suffer and the individuals on the team will be disgruntled. Finally, if the needs of the individuals are not met, no one will be focused on the task, the team will suffer and the task won't be executed as well as expected. Adair's eight rules for motivating people are:

1. Be motivated yourself
2. Select motivated people
3. Treat each person as an individual
4. Set realistic but challenging targets
5. Understand that progress itself motivates
6. Create a motivating environment
7. Provide relevant rewards
8. Recognise success

Each situation will, of course, be different, just as each individual will be. This is why we'd add a further element to the list, which is:

9. Motivate according to the circumstances

---

29 John Adair, *Action-Centred Leadership* (Farnborough, England: Gower Publishing Ltd, 1979). Professor John Adair is a leadership expert and author of more than forty books on business and leadership. www.adair-international.com; www.johnadair.co.uk.

MOTIVATE ACCORDING TO THE CIRCUMSTANCES

Alex Ferguson, ex-manager of Manchester United, who has been called the greatest football coach in history, is famed for his 'hairdryer' treatment of players who let him down. The media and commentators made much of the effectiveness of his ferocious half-time and post-game talks. But the reality was actually far more nuanced. Ferguson always worked hard to tailor his words to the situation. If, say, he had to tell a player he was being dropped for the next game, he would always do it privately and choose his words carefully. He'd say something like, 'I may be making a mistake here, but I think this is the best team for today.' He'd then follow up with some words to build their confidence, telling them it was a purely tactical decision and bigger games were coming up. During training sessions, his approach was to emphasise the positive. Plus, contrary to his reputation, he didn't always resort to the hairdryer if the team lost. If an individual player had given his best, that would be acknowledged. Of course, if anyone hadn't, well, they'd need to brace themselves.

A perfect example of this lies in Ferguson's dealings with the Manchester United player Dimitar Berbatov, who was constantly criticised in the media for being lazy and sloppy in his style. Yet, he was the Premier League's top goal scorer in the 2010–11 season. Not surprisingly, he had Ferguson's full support for his apparently laid-back playing style. The football manager understood that while it might not have looked particularly dynamic, what Berbatov was doing was lulling defenders into a false sense of security. Then, when he saw an opening, he was right on it, long before his opponents could react. It was his style, and it worked.[30]

Contrary to his reputation, Ferguson's overriding philosophy was that no one likes to be constantly criticised. Few people get better with criticism, and most people respond better to encouragement. 'Well done' can be a pretty powerful phrase. By the same token, no one wants or needs unnecessary praise when they know they have not done their best. A leader needs to point out mistakes and moments when individuals don't meet expectations.

Engagement and motivation are not static. People and situations change. All the time. Think back to your own experience as you weighed up what to do for a career. It's a fair bet that what you imagined at 18 years old was vastly different from what you want out of your career today. I had a vastly different view of life in my late teens. I wanted to get out, see the world and have fun, while experiencing some responsibility and variety. I joined the army and that is exactly what it gave me. As I have grown older, I have become more focused on my responsibilities and on bringing stability and support to my family. My motivations have changed and matured as time has gone on. Leaders need to keep checking in with their teams to find out where the mood is shifting. It can't be a one-size-fits-all affair – year in, year out. Plus, you can't judge others by your own values.

Finding out what motivates each member of the team needs to be part of the culture. Make it a regular habit to ask reports

---

30 Anita Elberse, 'Ferguson's Formula' (*Harvard Business Review*, October 2013), https://hbr.org/2013/10/fergusons-formula.

to finish meetings by showing, say, a YouTube clip of something that they find inspiring. Ask a different person to contribute each time and leave some room for discussion afterwards. It doesn't need to be a huge deal. It is not a formal presentation. It is, however, surprising how much this process reveals. Little events like this are great for perking up the whole team too.

It could even be a historic speech. Roderic cites this passage from a speech by Theodore Roosevelt, known as 'The Man in the Arena', as his most significant source of inspiration:

> 'It is not the critic who counts; not the man who points out how the strong man stumbles, or where the doer of deeds could have done them better. The credit belongs to the man who is actually in the arena, whose face is marred by dust and sweat and blood; who strives valiantly; who errs, who comes short again and again, because there is no effort without error and shortcoming; but who does actually strive to do the deeds; who knows great enthusiasms, the great devotions; who spends himself in a worthy cause; who at the best knows in the end the triumph of high achievement, and who at the worst, if he fails, at least fails while daring greatly, so that his place shall never be with those cold and timid souls who neither know victory or defeat.'[31]

CREATE AN ENVIRONMENT OF PSYCHOLOGICAL SAFETY

In any organisation, whether the team is scattered around the world or together in a tight-knit office, there needs to be good

---

31 Theodore Roosevelt, 'Citizenship in a Republic' (speech at the Sorbonne, Paris, 23 April 1910).

communication. The tone and delivery of this communication are crucial to engagement and motivation. For the team to be completely effective, there needs to be an environment where everyone feels free to share, or say, whatever they want, without fear that they are going to be criticised for it. In *The Culture Code: The Secrets of Highly Successful Groups*, author Daniel Coyle discusses the concept of creating an environment of psychological safety.[32] His research shows that the three skills at the heart of great teamwork are building safety, so everyone is comfortable in working together; creating a culture where people are allowed to show vulnerability, because no one needs to be perfect; and establishing purpose through common goals and a clear path to get there. If you think about it, being able to speak your mind freely is crucial when it comes to teamwork. No one will be proactive or creative if they feel they have to watch their back all the time.

Showing vulnerability does not come naturally to most people and that is doubly so in the workplace. It is seen as a weakness. This has a lot to do with corporate culture in the Western world, where those in senior positions need to be seen to be powerful all the time. In reality, vulnerability is a sign of strength, not weakness. Generally, a person who is willing to show they are not perfect at certain things, or who is willing to be proven wrong, wins instant respect – certainly, a lot more so than leaders who perpetually throw their weight around, bark orders or even berate others for being weak. Showing vulnerability also encourages others to show theirs. When this

---

32 Daniel Coyle, *The Culture Code: The Secrets of Highly Successful Groups* (London: Cornerstone, 2018).

happens, the parties become closer and trust each other more. It also signals a culture where making mistakes is okay. No one is perfect and that's fine.

The clear, overarching goal that we've talked about is the other component in creating a place of psychological safety. The goal is in the future and, obviously, everyone is in the here and now, but a clearly articulated purpose acts like a bridge between the two. When a leader comes up with a simple narrative about how the team will go from today to tomorrow and reach the goal, it motivates everyone into action. When the team feels safe, able to be vulnerable and allowed to make mistakes within the boundaries of that clear goal, good things happen. Today, many organisations are quite rightly trying to diversify their leadership teams. This is important since organisations should represent the people they seek to serve. But it's no good having a highly diverse workforce if they don't feel they can openly share their views or speak freely because the leadership has created conditions where it is not safe to do so.

All organisations should be working towards a culture of what humanistic psychologist Carl Rogers called 'unconditional positive regard', which is the basic acceptance and support of another person, regardless of what they say or do.[33] Even if other team members passionately disagree with a point of view, they should give their colleagues a fair hearing. They may be surprised by what they hear if they take the time to properly understand their interlocutor's arguments before making a judgement.

---

33 Saul McLeod, 'Carl Rogers' (*Simply Psychology*, 2014), https://www.simplypsychology.org/carl-rogers.html.

Roderic tells an interesting story about a woman who worked under deep cover for the CIA, infiltrating the Taliban in Afghanistan. Something that one member of the fundamentalist political and military organisation said to her really stopped her short and made her think about things differently. The representative she was speaking with questioned why the Americans were so quick to dismiss everyone in the movement as terrorists. Why then, he asked, were Americans always so in thrall of films such as those of the *Star Wars* franchise, where a plucky group of under-resourced rebels go up against an evil empire that has taken hold in their territory? Who is who in the Taliban versus US situation? When you look at the conflict from this viewpoint, it does open up new scenarios. You may still disagree passionately with the Taliban representative, but you may also understand a little of where they are coming from.

GIVE GOOD FEEDBACK

Feedback is, of course, an integral part of the communication process with any team and, indeed, in perfecting the balance shown in any of the spectrums in Part One. If you are seeking true engagement and motivation, as well as to make meaningful progress, it can't always be of the 'wow, you were brilliant and smashed it out of the park' type. Sooner or later, someone on the team is going to do something badly or make a huge mistake. That's fine. In fact, you have been working towards creating the environment for exactly this to happen in order to progress the whole organisation.

However, in order for feedback to be a learning opportunity, any mistakes need to be aired in the open, rather than quietly brushed under the carpet and ignored. But how does a leader give feedback without alienating their charges or ensuring that the charges never, ever stretch themselves again for fear of further negative reports?

What everyone needs to understand about feedback is that our visceral response to it is hardwired from childhood. From the moment we took our first steps or spoke our first words and everyone in the family went bananas with joy, we learned to connect feedback, in this case praise, with our inner selves or personalities. This notion is then added to at every milestone. When we went to school we were given a gold star for neat handwriting or 'star of the week' for good behaviour. (*I am a star!*) It continues through all stages of education right up to degree level. It goes on into the workplace too where, say, a junior salesperson is rewarded and incentivised. The boss will jump in and say, 'Well done, you beat your target by a mile – have Friday afternoon off.' It's hardly surprising that we become conditioned to enjoy positive feedback. Equally, we wince when anyone says something that hurts our ego.

This instinctive connection between feedback and how we all perceive ourselves and our personal worth presents a real challenge for any leader. How do you give genuine feedback but not leave the person on the receiving end reeling in shock and dismay? (*Am I not a star?*) The key is to separate the personality from the performance. Leaders need to work with their teams to help them understand that feedback is not an attack on them as individuals or their character, but part of their development to help them get better. This means carefully shaping conversations to switch emphasis to the positive: *this is how we will get the best out of you.*

It is possible to be challenging and direct, but also to frame your words in an empathetic way that does not alienate individuals. A good way to begin any difficult feedback conversation is to create the context from the off. Be honest that it is not going to be a comfortable discussion, but emphasise that it is in no way a judgement on the person's character or general performance.

'We are going to have this conversation because I want to help you get better,' is a good starting point.

Setting the context like this reinforces the work that has already been done to create an environment of psychological safety. The individual who is about to receive the feedback will immediately become more calm and at ease, and therefore more receptive to the message that is about to be delivered.

When giving the subsequent feedback, be wary of saying anything that may hint at an attack on their character, such as, 'You were totally unprepared for that meeting. You need to start putting more effort in.' That will instantly put the individual back on their guard, or, worse still, cause permanent damage to the relationship. Try instead something like: 'How do you think that meeting went? Do you think there is anything you could have done better?'

Focus the conversation on the performance, not the person who gave that performance.

It's always a good idea to follow up the day after a feedback conversation like this. Acknowledge that it was a tough discussion but emphasise that you believe in the individual and know that they will be going on to better things.

Say something like: 'I have full faith in your potential.'

Feedback is integral to achieving balance for both a leader and members of the team. If we don't have good, honest and open feedback, then we won't know if we are getting things right. It's up to a leader to create an environment where this can happen.

Nothing motivates and unifies talent more than a big goal. Challenge a team by setting big goals and maintain the momentum with regular feedback. They will naturally use their own best talents to contribute to a solution. Balance is, as always, essential. Be flexible in how you let everyone find their way of achieving the goal, because if a team is led too tightly, there is a risk that it will become insular and inflexible. However, don't let it go too far the other way either. If everyone is left to just get on with things, they may fall into the trap of becoming endlessly creative without every achieving anything in particular. Take care, too, that you don't load too much on the shoulders of each individual, or put them in a situation where they feel overwhelmed: everyone needs to recognise that they are working as a team and can rely on their colleagues. Most of all, though, if you invest more in your people, you will have a better business. Give something back to your team and they will give back to you. Engaged and motivated employees own their engagement with pride, and enjoy being a driving force.

AFTERWORD

When it comes to leadership, Roderic and I have long taken issue with the authenticity movement. Here, those in charge have done a Myers–Briggs or some other sort of personality or leadership test, and it has told them that they are an X, Y or Z personality. That is the sort of leader they are. Sadly, that is as far as it goes. They wear their version of 'authentic leadership' like a badge of honour that says: *this is who I am*. In reality, it simply seems to create a brilliant excuse for them not to change their behaviour according to different circumstances.

Leadership is, or at least should be, all about malleability according to the context. It is like the way water shapes itself to fit the environment into which it is poured, whether it is a glass, a bathtub or an ice cube tray. The interesting thing here is that water never stops being water. It doesn't change what it is as a substance; it just adapts itself to change its shape at a particular moment in time. The authenticity here is that water is always water. It doesn't pretend to be oil.

Leadership is an art, not a science. It is the art of balancing yourself and every part of the organisation you lead to meet the present context. To become an outstanding leader, you need to be able to immediately understand and sum up each new context and all the many variables. These variables may be anything and everything from the environment you are operating in to your own skills, the history of the issue or the make-up of the team, and many more besides. There will be times when the context changes dramatically and times when the changes are quite subtle, yet it is still important that you register that change and react to it. This may mean stepping in to take full control, while at other times the better option might be to give more responsibility to individual team members to handle the new circumstance. Often, a leader will need to be challenging, but equally, the situation might call for a bit of humility.

Balanced leadership is not always instinctive. You won't 'just know' the right place to be on any of the balance spectrums, whether it is pursuing the big picture or getting down into the detail, or sticking to process or letting the creative juices flow. To be able to operate at both ends of the spectrum, you need to learn and develop skills. Judgement is crucial, as are focus and clarity about the goal. Most of all, though, a leader needs to know how to take their team with them as they shift course and adjust their balance as necessary. To be effective, the relationship needs to be strong and based on a firm foundation of trust. Just as a leader needs to recognise their own strengths and weaknesses, they also need to respond to those of individuals on the team. It is only then that they will get full engagement and everyone pushing hard towards the big goal.

Often, learning how to use these skills will require trial and error – seeing what works and what doesn't. Many skills require practice, which means doing them over and over again until they come naturally. Some will even require you to build up to them, until you are able to achieve them properly. Even once you know the basics, it's good to pause now and again for a moment of careful reflection before jumping in and doing what you think needs to be done. Occasionally, a step back helps to reveal a very different picture, which requires a very different response.

Finding balance begins with finding out who you are and what your natural style is. You may naturally err towards the command-and-control style of leadership, or prefer to be more collegial. We are all born with different talents and are slightly better in some respects than in others. Just as some people are better athletes than others, or are more skilled at maths, you will have strong skills in some areas but be weaker in others. It is what we do with the talents that we were born with, and how we develop the ones that we are not so certain about, that shapes our leadership style and indicates whether we are good or great leaders.

Find your natural place on the leadership spectrums outlined here. When you know how you would normally react, think about whether or not it is appropriate in all circumstances. There is a very high probability that it is not. Once you understand this, you are on the way to making a deliberate choice to operate elsewhere on the spectrum when required.

As a leader, you will be constantly learning and adapting. It is impossible to reach a perfect balance and then stop right there. Balance will change all the time. There is no situation where you can afford to think: *I've got it just right. I am done.* Things change all the time and so should your response to them. It never stops. Likewise, our learning never stops. There are always new skills for a leader to acquire and that goes for the team too.

Balanced leadership is a craft that you need to develop and work on every single day.

For speeches and workshops relating
to content in *The Balanced Leader*,
please contact
info@balancedleaders.co.uk

ABOUT THE AUTHORS

Tim McEwan is a leadership advisor, mentor and coach. He started his career in the British Army, commissioning from the world-renowned Royal Military Academy Sandhurst. Tim's final role in the Army was as a Leadership Instructor at Sandhurst. Since leaving the Army, Tim has held numerous  leadership positions in business, and in 2015 was appointed a Fellow in Management Practice at the University of Cambridge's Judge Business School where he collaborates with the Executive Education department. Tim is also a passionate offshore and ocean sailor and skipper.

Roderic Yapp is an executive coach and leadership development specialist. A former Royal Marines Officer, he specialises in developing leaders that operate in highly demanding and competitive sectors. His experience includes the delivery of leadership development programmes across a multitude of  sectors, including professional services, banking, insurance, pharmaceuticals and professional sport.

CPSIA information can be obtained
at www.ICGtesting.com
Printed in the USA
LVHW041249121221
705979LV00013B/1809